Laurence A. Connors & Blake E. Hayward

Investment Secrets of a Hedge Fund Manager

Exploiting the Herd Mentality of the Financial Markets

PROBUS
PUBLISHING

Chicago, Illinois
Cambridge, England

ISBN 1-55738-900-4

Printed in the United States of America

BB

1 2 3 4 5 6 7 8 9 0

JB

To Karen, Brittany, and Alexandra,
my parents, Irving and Barbara Connors,
and my grandparents, Manuel and Rose Gordon.

— L.C.

To my parents, Roger and Rosalie Hayward.

— B.H.

Disclaimer

It should not be assumed that the methods, techniques, or indicators presented in this book will be profitable or that they will not result in losses. Past results are not necessarily indicative of future results. It should not be assumed that the authors traded any of the examples in this book. Examples are for educational purposes only. This is not a solicitation of any order to buy or sell.

The NFA requires us to state that "HYPOTHETICAL OR SIMULATED PERFORMANCE RESULTS HAVE CERTAIN INHERENT LIMITATIONS. UNLIKE AN ACTUAL PERFORMANCE RECORD, SIMULATED RESULTS DO NOT REPRESENT ACTUAL TRADING. ALSO, SINCE THE TRADES HAVE NOT ACTUALLY BEEN EXECUTED, THE RESULTS MAY HAVE UNDER-OR-OVER COMPENSATED FOR THE IMPACT, IF ANY, OF CERTAIN MARKET FACTORS, SUCH AS LACK OF LIQUIDITY. SIMULATED TRADING PROGRAMS IN GENERAL ARE ALSO SUBJECT TO THE FACT THAT THEY ARE DESIGNED WITH THE BENEFIT OF HINDSIGHT. NO REPRESENTATION IS BEING MADE THAT ANY ACCOUNT WILL OR IS LIKELY TO ACHEIVE PROFITS OR LOSSES SIMILAR TO THOSE SHOWN."

Trademarks

The following are trademarks held by Oceanview Financial Research, Inc.:

Connors-Hayward Advance-Decline Trading Pattern (CHADTP)
Connors-Hayward Historical Volatility System
News Reversals
Undeniables

Table of Contents

Preface

A few weeks ago, my wife Karen came into my office and told me she finally figured out why Blake and I were writing this book.

My wife is a cooking fanatic and watches cooking shows on television whenever possible. She had just watched a show hosted by a well-known personality in the cooking industry. Without naming names, this woman is famous for one of her foods, and rich enough from this food to buy and sell most of us.

After a few moments of watching this program, it was apparent to my wife that this woman did not know how to cook. The woman made mistake after mistake in describing how to cook a simple recipe. My wife asked herself, how could someone who did not even know how to cook, claim to be such an expert?

We ask the same question about many authors of trading books. The financial rewards from the markets is enormous, yet most authors of investment books don't trade. A publisher of a major financial publishing house told us that more than 90 percent of the trading books on the market today are written by individuals who do not trade for a living. Though many of these people profess to be in possession of the holy grail, their primary income is derived from sources outside of trading.

This book is written by two people whose financial survival is dependent upon successfully trading the markets. This does not mean we have all the answers. It only means we have the knowledge and guts to put our money where our mouths are. This book is written for the trader who is looking to become successful. Those of you looking for a book that is full of financial theory will be disappointed. We have attempted to show the reader our trading strategies as simply as possible with as many examples as possible. Those of you counting on our strategies working 100 percent of the time will also be disappointed. We show the losing trades along with the winners.

All of the strategies in this book are proprietary. Many of our strategies attempt to exploit market psychology at extreme points. Finally, all of our strategies are market neutral. This means they should work in bull markets, bear markets, and most importantly sideways markets.

Some people have asked us if we were afraid of too many people trading our strategies. While this would be the ultimate compliment, the trading community is made up of intelligent people who will not copy someone word for word. Most traders will implement their own twists and turns and fine-tune a trading strategy to fit their personality. This we know from personal experience, and we encourage it.

Finally, we hope you profit from this book. If after completing it you have just learned one new trading strategy, we will consider our efforts a success.

Acknowledgments

The indebtedness we have to the following individuals cannot be fully described in words. All helped in the making of this book, and all contributed immensely.

Kevin Commins and the staff at Probus Publishing—For taking a chance on two first-time writers.

Derek Gipson—For his invaluable assistance and input on our trading strategies.

Janice Hayward—For her assistance, especially for reading and critiquing our entire manuscript.

Sheldon Natenberg—For his invaluable input with the historical volatility chapter.

Jared Wise—For doing the grunt work behind the research. You have a bright future ahead of you.

Kevin Armstrong, Vito Chieco, and the rest of the crew on the Z-desk at Lind-Waldock—Great fills. Great service. What else could a trader ask for?

To our fellow directors Dr. Joseph Bassett and Dr. Paul Ruggieri—For helping make the dream a reality and most importantly for their friendship.

Chapter One

-
-
-
-
-

The Herd

For, whether the prize be a ribbon or throne
the victor is he who can go it alone.

John Godfrey Saxe

October 5, 1994—The market has sold off more than 200 points over the past three weeks. Analysts are calling for it to drop another 200 points. The gurus are saying this is the beginning of a new bear market. The logical thing to do is sell your stocks and short the market. Six trading days later, the Dow Jones Industrial Average is trading 130 points higher.

October 8, 1993—Gambling fever is sweeping the nation. Investors cannot buy enough gambling stocks. Every gaming analyst on Wall Street is recommending their purchase. The Gambling Stock Index has appreciated more than 50 percent over the last nine months, yet every gaming analyst on Wall Street continues to recommend these stocks. Seven weeks later the index has dropped 15 percent, and the October 1993 highs are not seen again.

June 3, 1994—The Japanese yen has been moving sideways for weeks. Most analyst and traders are saying they see no reason for the yen to move either up or down. Two trading days later, the yen is up over one cent, and within three weeks it trades to its highest level ever.

Why did these markets move the way they did when the common wisdom was predicting the opposite? The easiest way to answer this is to look at the function of the specialist on the New York Stock Exchange.

Some of the biggest winners at this game are the specialists. Just look at their job. Their job is to buy stocks when everyone is selling and to sell stocks when everyone is buying. When everyone is buying, it is obviously because events are positive; and when everyone is selling, it is obviously because events are bad. Logically, the people who invest for these reasons should be the winners, not the specialists, yet this is not the case. It has been reported that the average specialist firm achieves returns in excess of 40 percent—year in and year out. They are consistently on the opposite side of the herd and on the opposite side of the so-called "logic."

The biggest fortunes on Wall Street and the futures market are made by individuals who know how to exploit the herd mentality of the marketplace. These people are known as contrarians, but being a contrarian is only one piece of the puzzle. It is also critical to have a specific trading strategy to exploit the markets and a trading methodology that works in all markets.

Too many trading plans work in only one type of market. The best plans work in all markets. An example is the system used by a well-known money manager in the late 1970s through the mid-1980s. This individual made a fortune using a strategy that was basically a congestion breakout system. In the years that he made his millions, the markets had some major trends. Unfortunately for this individual and his disciples, the late 80s and early 90s saw markets that were filled with false breakouts and extended periods of congestion. Things were so bad for his methodology that he was forced to retire from the money management business. This example is not meant to downgrade this trader's achievements. He achieved more success in a decade than most traders achieve in a lifetime. The lesson to be learned is that he did not have a strategy that exploited the markets as they were behaving in the late 80s and early 90s.

The same scenario is true on Wall Street. Strategies come in and out of favor. In the 1980s value investing was the fad. Cash flow and breakup value was king. This ended in 1989. Since that time, momentum investing has become the fad. Buy the stocks that make new highs; sell the laggards. We suspect that this fad will also pass.

Other fads come and go. Biotechnology stocks were the craze from late 1990 to early 1992. As a group, prices appreciated over 150 percent during that time. The 28-year-old money manager for Fidelity's biotechnology fund was hailed as a financial genius by the press. Money poured into these stocks. Predictably, the prices of the biotechnology stocks plunged over the next 12 months, and many of those who bought stock in these companies in late 1991 are still holding onto losses today. These investors, unfortunately, had a strategy that was solely dependent upon a bull market in a particular sector.

The strategies you will learn in this book are not market dependent. The strategies combined will allow you ample opportunity to profit from bull markets, bear markets, and sideways markets. We have put together strategies that we believe exploit markets that are going through various psychological stages. These strategies have been historically tested and are the strategies we use on a daily basis. Finally, these are the strategies you would have used to exploit the three examples at the beginning of this chapter.

The strategies in this book are built upon our belief that human emotions are at times irrational. We have attempted to apply historically proven methods to exploit this irrational behavior for financial gains. Also, the techniques we present are short-term in nature. We do not believe market direction can be accurately predicted over longer periods of time. Finally, the trading methodology taught in this book is unique. This will give you the edge over the horde of traders who continue to use the same old, worn-out strategies.

Before we go further, we need to say a word on opinions. The futures markets and Wall Street are filled with opinions. Unfortunately, individual opinions are nothing more than educated guesses. The premise behind our methodology is the belief that one's opinion cannot be quantified and is therefore useless in predicting market direction.

The book is laid out as follows:

Chapter 2, **News Reversals**, is our favorite chapter. This chapter will teach you how to identify times that the herd miscalculates the effects of news stories. The potential profits from this strategy in the futures and equity markets are great and come quickly.

Chapter 3, **Connors-Hayward Historical Volatility System**, contains one of the most exciting indicators we trade. This chapter will teach you how to identify markets that are about to explode. While everyone is ignoring these markets, you will be anticipating a market explosion. The potential profits from these moves is enormous. As far as we know, no one has ever used historical volatility as described in this book.

Chapter 4 is a strategy we call **Undeniables**. In this chapter, you will learn how to identify index sectors that are about to experience short- and intermediate-term trend changes.

Chapter 5 is the **Connors-Hayward Advance-Decline Trading Pattern (CHADTP)**. Advance-decline lines have been used to measure overbought and oversold conditions in the stock market for years. Up until now, though, no one has used a specific entry point to successfully enter these markets when they reverse. In this chapter, you will learn how to identify overbought and oversold conditions and how to enter them successfully in order to exploit stock market panic and euphoria at their extremes.

Chapter 6, **New Markets, New Indicators**, will teach you how to trade the Globex markets, how to use the VIX indicator and how the NASDAQ 100 Index acts as a leading indicator for the S&P 500 futures market and Dow Jones Industrial Average.

In Chapters 7 and 8, **Why Most Traders Lose** and **Survival of the Fittest**, you will learn the money management strategies and the psychology you need to become a top trader.

Finally, Chapter 9, **Putting It All Together,** will touch on how to put together a trading plan using this book's methodologies.

Now onto the trading strategies . . .

Chapter Two

-
-
-
-
-

News Reversals™

Look before you leap.

Anonymous

One of our most exciting and profitable trading methods occurs when markets gap higher on bullish news or gap lower on bad news and reverse. We call this trading method *news reversals*, because it requires a major news event to trigger a signal. This trading strategy is the epitome of exploiting the herd mentality.

For example, let's look at a hypothetical situation in the soybean market. After the market closes, a crop report is released that shows a shortage of soybeans, which is bullish for soybean prices. Analysts and experts then go out and make very positive statements about the report. A buying frenzy is created before the opening, causing prices to gap higher. This gap opening creates a short-term overbought condition. Prices, instead of moving higher as expected, begin moving lower. This selling begets further selling. Commercials come into the market to lock into prices that are higher than yesterday. Short sellers begin to smell blood and push prices even lower. The speculators who believed prices could only go higher begin to panic. A full-blown sell-off occurs, and prices head much lower. The trading strategy to exploit this scenario can make an individual thousands of dollars very quickly.

Here are the rules:

Rule #1: Traders should wait for an extremely bullish or bearish event to occur after the market has closed. For futures traders, this can be a crop report, livestock report, economic report, weather report, and so on. Equity traders should be looking at earnings reports, takeover rumors, brokerage house recommendations, and so on.

Rule # 2: The market must gap open above or below the previous day's high or low for a signal to occur.

Rule #3: On openings that gap higher, place a sell stop one tick below the previous day's high. On openings that gap lower, place a buy stop one tick above the previous day's low. Note: Equities cannot be purchased via buy stops. The order must be done manually.

Rule #4: After you are filled, stops should be placed at the morning's opening price. As prices move in your favor, stops should be adjusted to lock into profits.

The following examples help illustrate why we find this trading strategy so profitable.

Example #1. This example is one of our favorites because it sets itself up perfectly.

On November 8, 1994, political history is made as the Republicans gain control of both the Senate and the House of Representatives for the first time in 40 years. The next morning, the dollar and bond markets surges on the news. A buying panic for stocks is created before the opening. "Tax cuts . . . less federal regulation . . . buy drug and defense stocks" is the rallying cry before the opening. A news service quotes one market strategist as predicting the Dow will open 25 points higher. A few minutes later, another strategist is quoted as predicting the Dow will open at least 35 points higher.

At 9:30 A.M. (EST), the S&P 500 gaps open 4.65 points higher, and within nine minutes the Dow Jones Industrial Average is up 38 points on enormous volume. Half of our news reversal pattern has been set up. As happens so many times, the market's euphoria turns into

Example I

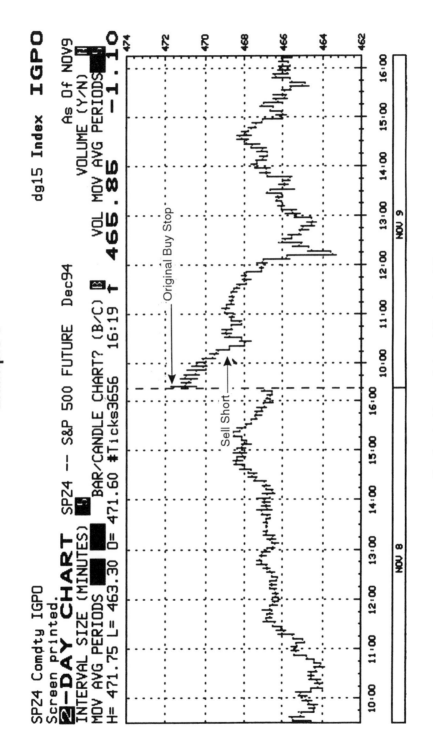

Reprinted with permission of Bloomberg L.P.

doom. Instead of continuing its advance, the market begins to sell off. A sell-short order is triggered at 468.70, one tick below the previous day's high. A buy-stop order for protection is placed at the day's opening price of 471.60. The market moves sideways for about an hour before the next wave of selling hits. The S&P 500 finds itself down more than 8 points from the high made 2 1/2 hours earlier. The Dow, which had been up almost 40 points, is now down more than 20 points.

Depending on the trailing stop-order strategy one employs, a trader could net over a $2,500 per contract profit in less than 90 minutes.

Example #2. The coffee market went through a major bull market in 1994 due to drought fears.

On Monday October 17, the December contract for the coffee market is called to open 5–7 cents lower due to the rains that have occurred over the weekend. Coffee in fact opens down 9.35 cents from Friday's close and immediately reverses. A buy stop is placed at 185.80, one tick above Friday's low. At 11:40 (EST), a news reversal buy signal is triggered. Immediately, a sell stop is placed at 179.00 (the day's opening.) The market explodes upward 20 minutes later and closes at 203.85 for a day trading profit of a little more than $6,750 per contract.

Example 2

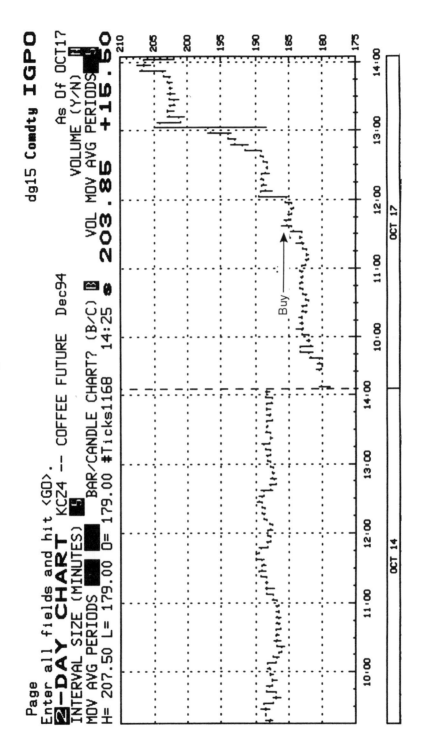

Example #3. Before the soybean market opens on October 20, 1994, the National Weather Service reports that drier weather is expected. The drier weather will allow farmers to resume harvesting their fields after a rain delay earlier in the week. November Soybeans gap down to 539.60. A buy stop is placed at 540.75, one tick above the previous day's low, and is executed shortly thereafter. Prices rally strongly and close at 549.50 for a 8 3/4 cents profit for the day.

Example 3

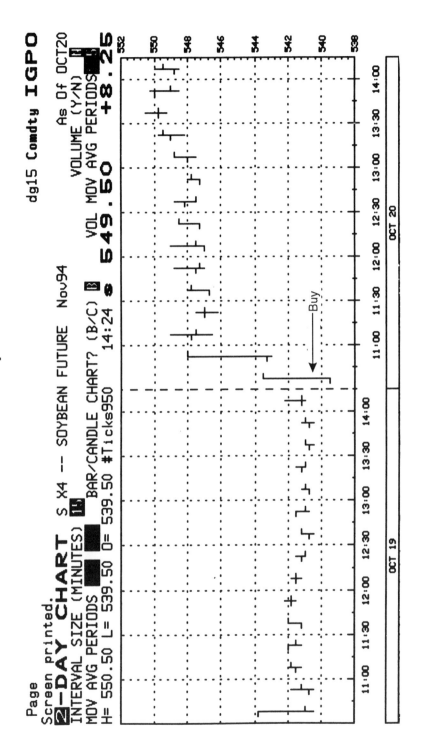

Reprinted with permission of Bloomberg L.P.

Example #4. On November 4, 1994, the stock market is called to open higher due to a better-than-expected employment report.

The December contract of the S&P gaps open to 470.20, 140 points above the previous day's close. A sell stop is placed at 469.75, one tick below the previous day's high. After the euphoria of the report subsides, the market reverses. The market continues to sell off and closes at 462.40, for a profit of more than $3,500 per contract.

Example 4

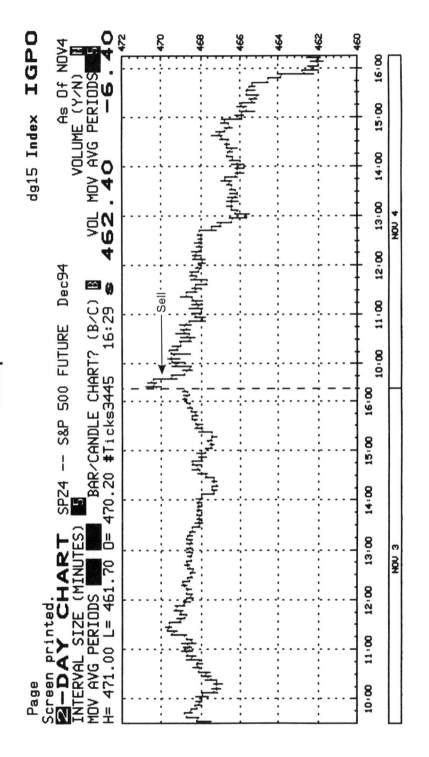

Reprinted with permission of Bloomberg L.P.

Example #5. After the close on October 12, 1994, the USDA reports that Florida orange growers will harvest a much larger crop than projected. The next morning, January orange juice opens at 94.00, down 2.35 cents from the previous day's close. A buy stop is placed at 94.35, one tick above the previous day's low. Almost immediately, the buy-stop order is filled, and a protective sell stop is placed at the day's opening price of 94.00. The market drifts higher for the next couple of hours and then explodes to as high as 99.75 cents before settling at 99.25 for a day trading profit of 4.90 cents.

The following three news reversal examples are from the equity markets.

Example 5

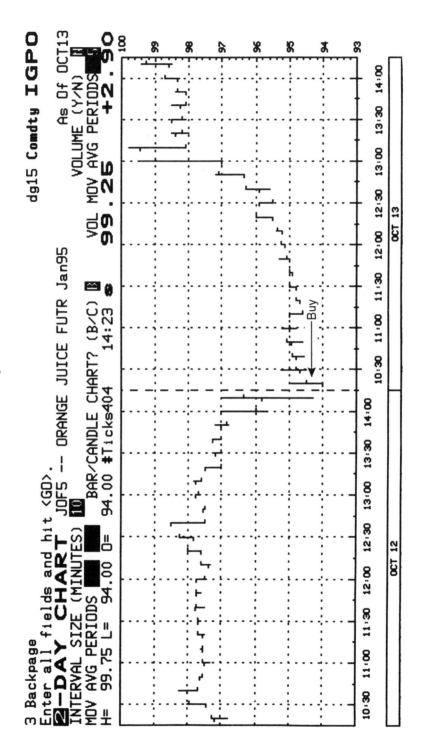

Reprinted with permission of Bloomberg L.P.

Example #6. Before the opening, on January 26, 1994, Clark Equipment, one of the largest construction machinery companies in the world, announces earnings below Wall Street's expectations. It takes the specialist almost 45 minutes to open the stock due to an imbalance of sell orders. The stock finally opens, down 1 1/8 to 50 1/4, and immediately reverses. A news reversal buy order is triggered at 51 3/8, 1/8 above the previous day's low of 51 1/4. At this point, those who had sold on the opening at 50 1/4 are feeling foolish, and the short sellers are feeling the pain. The stock continues to rise throughout the day and closes at 52 3/8, up 1 1/8 from the previous day's close. Over the next few days, the stock continues to rally and three days later closes at 58 3/8, seven points higher than the entry point.

Example 6

Reprinted with permission of Omega Research Inc.

Example #7. On October 8, 1993, Hoechst Celanese announces they are buying a 51 percent stake in Copley Pharmaceutical, a company whose stock price has tripled over the past 12 months. On Monday morning, October 11, Copley's stock opens at 53, 3 1/4 points above Friday's close. The market reverses and a short sale is made at 49 7/8 (1/8 below Friday's high of 50).

The short position will be covered at 53 (the day's opening) if we are wrong. The market continues to sell off, though, and closes at 46 for a day-trading profit of 3 7/8 points.

The long-term sell-off is more dramatic. After our news-reversal pattern, the stock loses an additional 24 points over the next four months.

Example 7

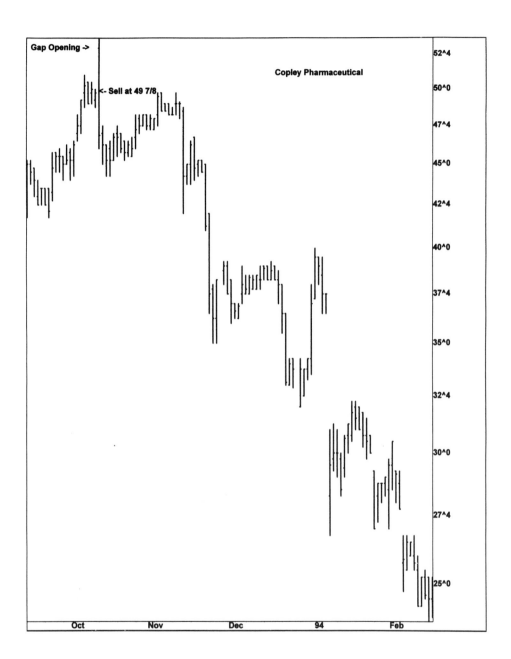

Reprinted with permission of Omega Research Inc.

Example #8. After the market closes on September 14, 1994, Federal Express announces earnings that far exceed Wall Street's expectations. The next morning, before the opening, a number of brokerage houses either raise their opinions or raise their earnings estimates for the company. After a 30-minute delay caused by an onslaught of buy orders, Federal Express opens 7/8 of a point higher than the previous day's high. A sell short stop is placed at 70 1/8, 1/8 of a point (one tick) below the previous day's high. The stock proceeds to trade as high as 72 1/8 and reverses, closing the day at 67 3/4, down 2 1/2 points for the day. The sell-off in Federal Express continues over the next three days, pushing the stock down an additional 7 3/4 points.

Example 8

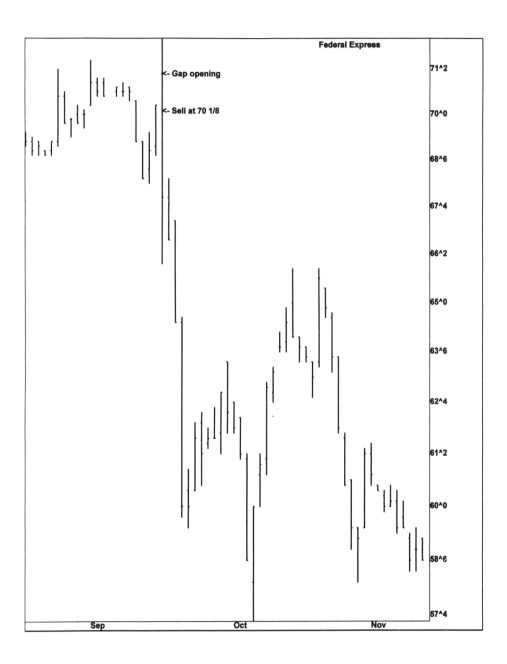

Reprinted with permission of Omega Research Inc.

SUMMARY

As you can see, news reversals can be a very profitable trading strategy. Obviously, not all gaps caused by news reverse themselves. However, when reversals do occur, the probability of them being profitable is high.

We have selected examples from the futures market over a five-week period that was very profitable. On the whole, our research has shown that news reversals, when traded correctly, can be profitable approximately 70 percent of the time. Because the potential impact of each news story is subjective, the results will vary slightly from trader to trader. Aggressive traders will take all news stories as a reason to trade this strategy. Conservative traders will be more patient and only trade those news stories they believe are significant.

The most important lesson of this chapter is this: If it doesn't go up on good news, it is going down; and if it doesn't go down on bad news, it is going up. News reversals prove it.

Chapter Three

-
-
-
-
-

Connors-Hayward Historical Volatility System™

The great mistake is to anticipate the outcome of the engagement.
Let nature take its course, and your tools will strike at the right moment.

Bruce Lee

We predict that the use of historical volatility will be one of the growth areas for research in the financial markets in the late 90s. Up until now, the use of historical volatility has been confined mostly to the options market, but we have found it can be equally applied to the futures and equities markets.

Historical volatility is defined as the standard deviation of day-to-day price change expressed as an annualized percentage. In simpler terms, it is the degree to which prices fluctuate over a period of time. The best way to explain this is with an example. If a stock is selling for $50 per share and has a one-year historical volatility reading of 10 percent, it means that 68 percent of the time at the end of a one-year period, the stock has traded between 45 and 55. A 10-day historical volatility reading would mean that over the past 10 days its annualized range would be between 45 and 55, 68 percent of the time (one standard deviation). (For further information on volatility and the calculations for historical volatility, please see the appendix.)

A high volatility reading means the underlying security is extremely volatile; whereas, a low volatility reading signals a lack of volatility.

As mentioned, most market participants use volatility readings to trade options. Professional traders attempt to buy historically cheap options and attempt to sell historically expensive volatility options. Our approach is different. We use historical volatility readings to signal major advances and declines for equities and futures. Our research has shown that whenever a 10-day historical volatility reading reaches half or less of its 100-day historical volatility reading, a major move for that market is nearing.

In his book, *Option Volatility and Pricing,* Sheldon Natenberg points out that volatility has a tendency to be mean-reverting. This means that a shorter-term volatility will have a tendency to correct itself back to its longer-term reading. For example, if the 100-day historical volatility is 30 percent and the 10-day historical volatility is 14 percent, the 10-day reading will eventually find its way back to 30 percent. For this to happen, the market must move strongly, and most often this move will be in one direction. By waiting for the 10-day volatility to drop to half or less of its 100-day reading, we are basically identifying a market where a great deal of complacency is occurring. While everyone else is asleep, ignoring this market, an explosion is about to occur.

Let us look at the following examples as further evidence of this phenomena. The first five examples will give you a better understanding of the potential of this indicator. Then we will go through a three-year period trade by trade for the currency markets (yen), the grain markets (soybeans), and a stock market sector index (Philadelphia gold and silver stock index).

Example #1. Our first example is from the Nikkei 225 index.

On May 13, 1994, the 10-day historical volatility (H.V.) for the Nikkei 225 drops to 10.90 percent while the 100-day H.V. is at 25.63 percent. Because the 10-day reading is less than half the 100-day read-

Example I—Nikkei 225 Index

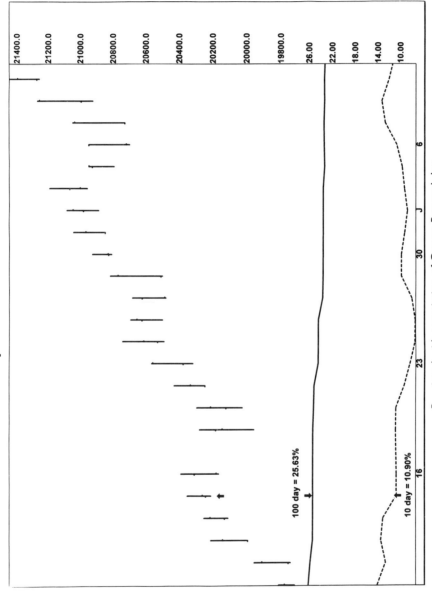

Reprinted with permission of Omega Research Inc.

ing, a signal is rendered, warning us that a large move is imminent. The Nikkei trades sideways for a couple of days before moving up over 1300 points over the next four weeks.

Example #2. Here's a stock example.

On August 28, 1994, Chiron, a biotechnology company, has a 10-day H.V. reading of 19.11 percent, while its 100-day reading is at 40.88 percent, thereby triggering a signal. Two trading days later, Chiron is up almost four points. Nine days later, it's over 12 points higher, for a 20 percent appreciation in two weeks.

Example 2—Chiron Corp.

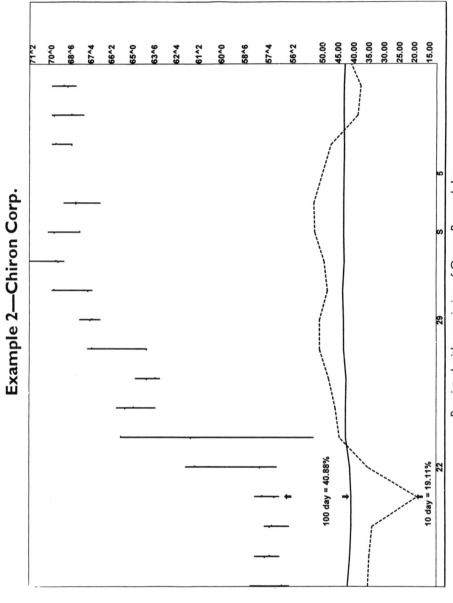

Reprinted with permission of Omega Research Inc.

Example #3. This example is from the computer technology index, which trades on the American Stock Exchange.

On September 28, 1994, the 10-day H.V. is at 8.00 percent, while the 100-day H.V. is at 17.26 percent. A few days later, the index bottoms at 142.92. Over the next four weeks, the index explodes more than 15 percent to 164.93.

Example 3—Computer Technology Index

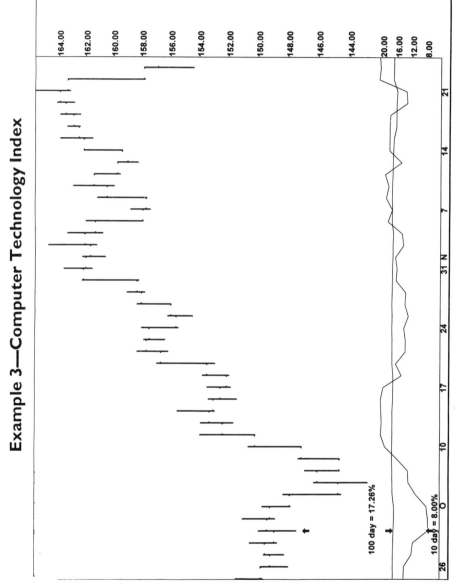

Reprinted with permission of Omega Research Inc.

Example #4. Though our indicator did not predict the crash of 87 (this is the only indicator in the world, by the way, that didn't predict the crash), it did predict the move that led to the 82–87 bull market high.

On July 17, 1987, the 10-day H.V. is at 7.97 percent, while the 100-day is at 16.45 percent. The Dow Jones Industrial Average opens at 2450 the next day and proceeds to rise over 286 points over the next six weeks, peaking out at 2736 on August 25, 1987!

Example 4—Dow Jones Industrial

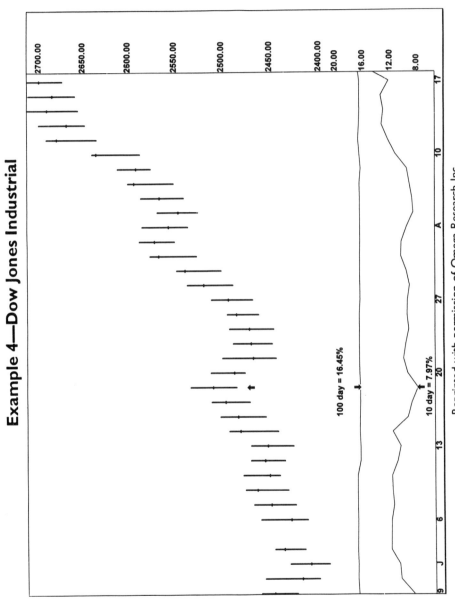

100 day = 16.45%

10 day = 7.97%

Reprinted with permission of Omega Research Inc.

We feel it is more convincing and more educational to look at an indicator on a day-by-day basis. Let's apply historical volatility to three different markets over a continuous period of time.

SOYBEANS: JANUARY 1, 1992 TO NOVEMBER 1, 1994

Example #1. February 27, 1992, the 10-day historical volatility reading is at 7.98 percent, while the 100-day H.V. reading is at 16.51 percent. Because the 10-day reading is less than half the 100-day reading, the potential for a near-term market explosion exists. On February 28, March soybeans open at 575 and trade as much as 28 cents higher over the next six trading days.

Example I—Soybeans

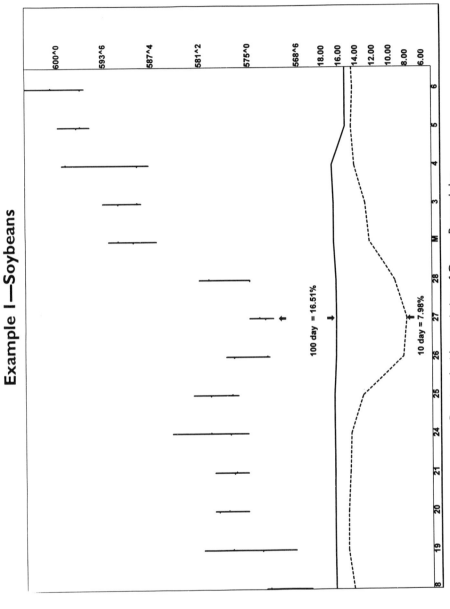

Reprinted with permission of Omega Research Inc.

Example #2. On July 20, the 10-day H.V. reading reaches 7.04 percent, while the 100-day H.V. reading is at 17.74 percent. September soybeans open the next day at 558 and trade sideways for the next seven trading sessions. On July 31, beans break sharply to the downside and trade to under 540 within three weeks.

Example 2—Soybeans

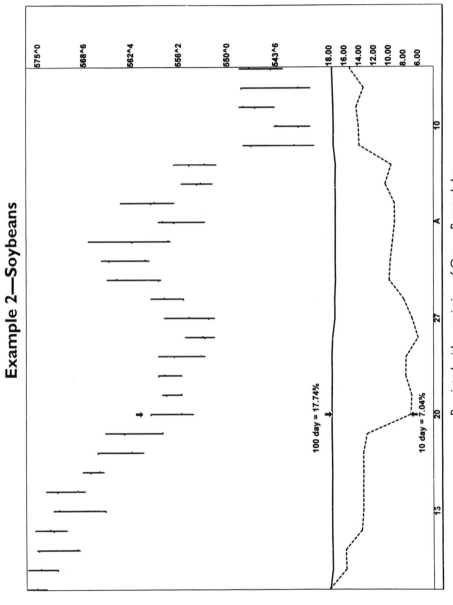

Reprinted with permission of Omega Research Inc.

Example #3. October 16, the 100-day H.V. is at 6.10 percent, while the 100-day is at 15.83 percent. The next day, soybeans are up seven cents for the day and continue to trend higher through the life of the contract.

Example 3—Soybeans

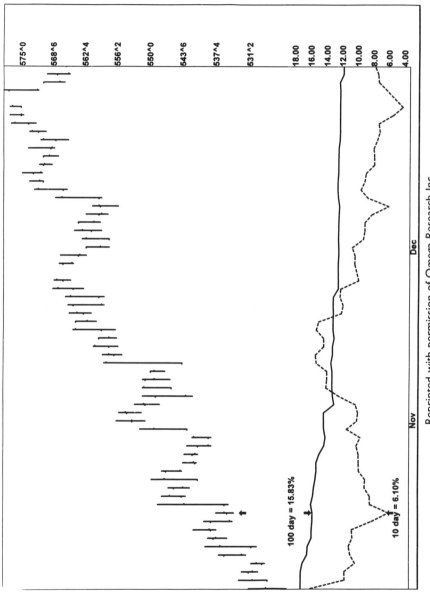

100 day = 15.83%

10 day = 6.10%

Nov

Dec

575^0
568^6
562^4
556^2
550^0
543^6
537^4
531^2
18.00
16.00
14.00
12.00
10.00
8.00
6.00
4.00

Reprinted with permission of Omega Research Inc.

Example #4. On December 8, 1992, the 10-day H.V. reading is 6.15 percent, and the 100-day is 12.48 percent. Over the next two days, the market rallies 12 cents and within a month is trading 20 cents higher.

Example 4—Soybeans

575^0	
572^4	
570^0	
567^4	
565^0	
562^4	
560^0	
557^4	
555^0	
15.00	
13.00	
11.00	
9.00	
7.00	
5.00	

100 day = 12.48%

10 day = 6.15%

Reprinted with permission of Omega Research Inc.

Example #5. This is the first signal in 10 months. On October 18, 1993, the 10-day H.V. reading is at 6.73 percent, while the 100-day H.V. reading is at 23.32 percent. Within days, the market moves to the upside and trades more than 60 cents higher within four weeks.

Example 5—Soybeans

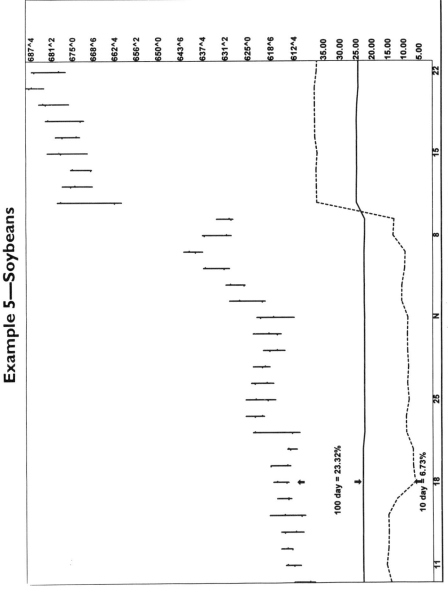

Reprinted with permission of Omega Research Inc.

Example #6. January 27, 1994, the 10-day H.V. reaches 9.24 percent, while the 100-day reading is at 20.38 percent. March beans open at 704 the next day and drop over 30 cents within seven trading sessions.

Example 6—Soybeans

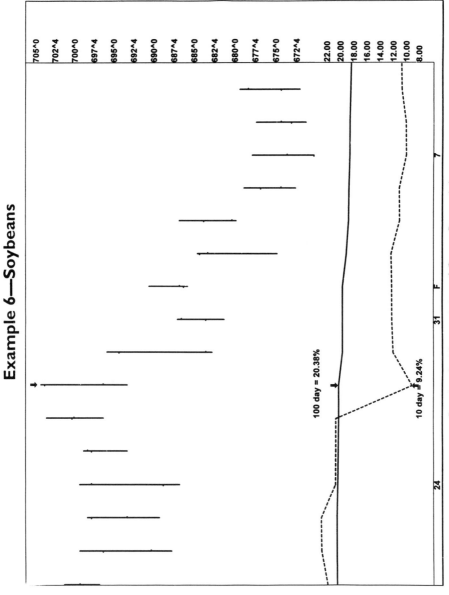

Reprinted with permission of Omega Research Inc.

Example #7. On August 4, 1994, a signal is triggered when a 10-day H.V. reading reaches 12.58 percent while the 100-day H.V. is at 25.70 percent. Within two days, September beans are up as much as 16 cents and over the next four weeks rise almost 30 cents.

Example 7—Soybeans

Reprinted with permission of Omega Research Inc.

Example #8. This signal occurred before a sharp sell-off in November soybeans.

On September 20, the 10-day H.V. is 12.43 percent and the 100-day H.V. is at 25.63 percent. The market begins selling off within a couple of days, losing a total of 20 cents in 2 1/2 weeks.

Example 8—Soybeans

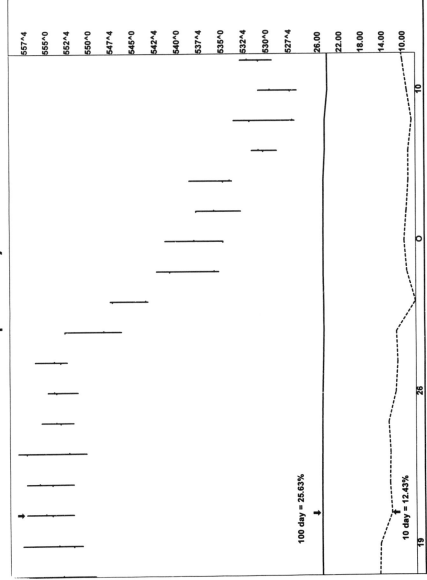

Reprinted with permission of Omega Research Inc.

JAPANESE YEN:
JANUARY 1, 1992 TO NOVEMBER 1, 1994

Example #1. The first signal occurs on February 20, 1992, on the March contract when the 10-day volatility reading drops to 5.64 percent and the 100-day volatility reading is at 11.57 percent. We know a major move is pending because the 10-day H.V. reading is less than half the 100-day H.V. reading. The next day, March yen opens at 77.57 and proceeds to sell-off three full cents over the next three weeks.

Example I—Yen

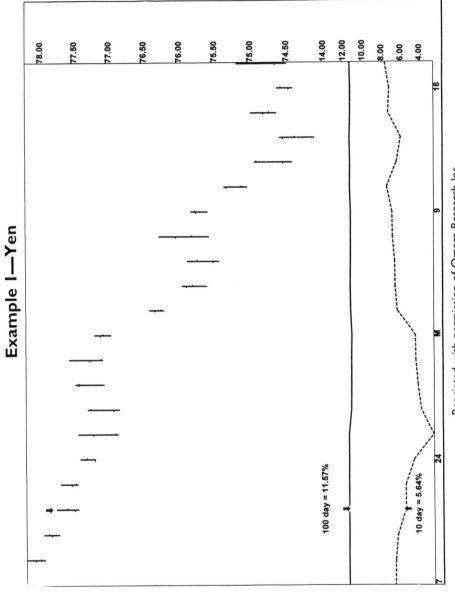

Reprinted with permission of Omega Research Inc.

Example #2. On April 24, after having traded sideways for almost six weeks, the June yen records a 10-day H.V. reading of 4.58 percent, while the 10-day H.V. reading is at 10.84 percent, thereby triggering a signal. The next trading day, the yen opens at 75.08 and moves higher by over 4 1/2 cents over the next seven weeks.

Example 2—Yen

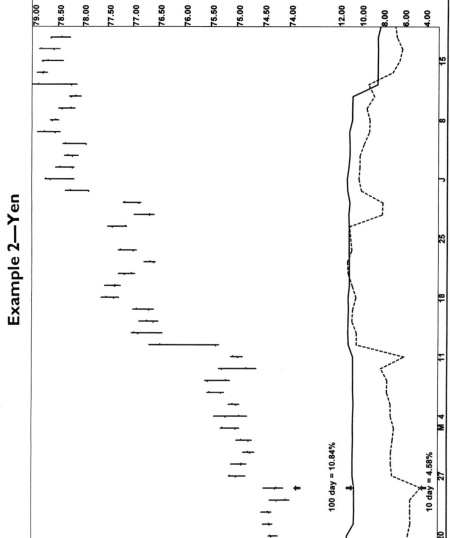

Reprinted with permission of Omega Research Inc.

Example #3. August 7, the 10-day H.V. is at 3.77 percent, while the 100-day is at 8.39 percent. The September yen is trading at 78.27 and within three days begins an ascent that brings it to as high as 81.77 over the next four weeks.

Example 3—Yen

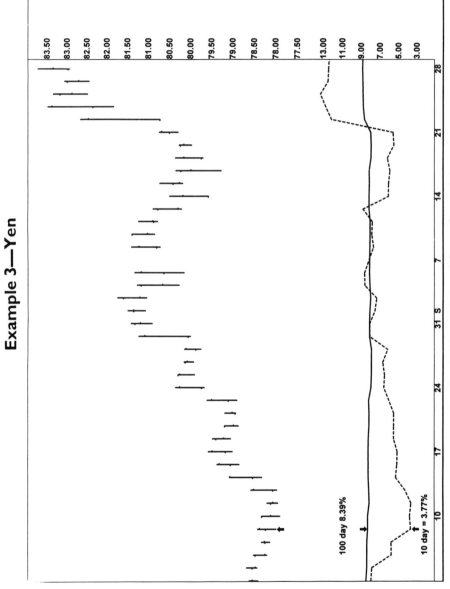

Reprinted with permission of Omega Research Inc.

Example #4. In early 1993, a signal is triggered on the yen when the 10-day H.V. reading reaches 4.17 percent and the 100-day H.V. reading is 9.13 percent. Over the next six weeks, the yen appreciates from under 80 cents to as high as 86 cents.

Example 4—Yen

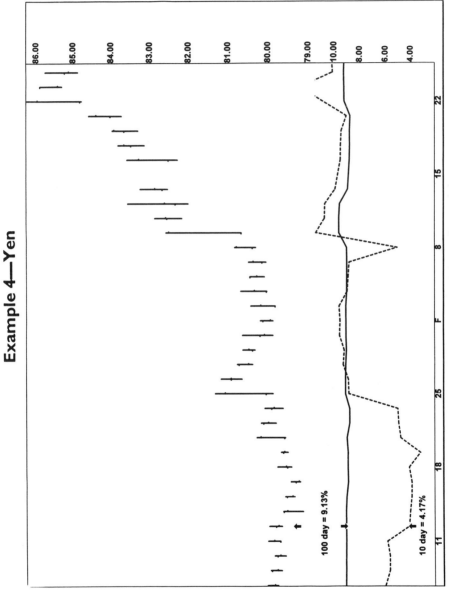

Reprinted with permission of Omega Research Inc.

Example #5. On October 5, 1993, the 10-day H.V. is at 7.39 percent, while the 100-day H.V. is at 14.87 percent. The market drops immediately and trades lower over the next two weeks.

Example 5—Yen

95.50
95.00
94.50
94.00
93.50
93.00
92.50
92.00
17.00
15.00
13.00
11.00
9.00
7.00

100 day = 14.87%

10 day = 7.39%

4   11   18   25

Reprinted with permission of Omega Research Inc.

Example #6. A false signal. On December 21, 1993, the 10-day H.V. is at 5.50 percent, and the 100-day is at 12.33 percent. The market trends sideways for the next three weeks.

Example 6—Yen

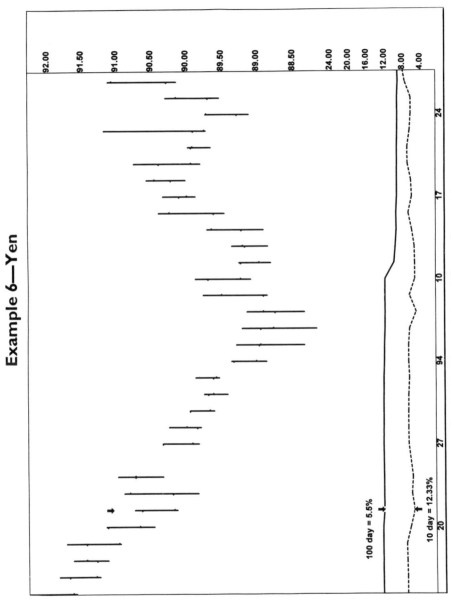

Reprinted with permission of Omega Research Inc.

Example #7. An immediate move from our signal. On June 2, 1994, the 10-day H.V. is at 5.78 percent, while the 100-day is at 13.20 percent. The market rallies as much as six cents over the next five weeks.

Example 7—Yen

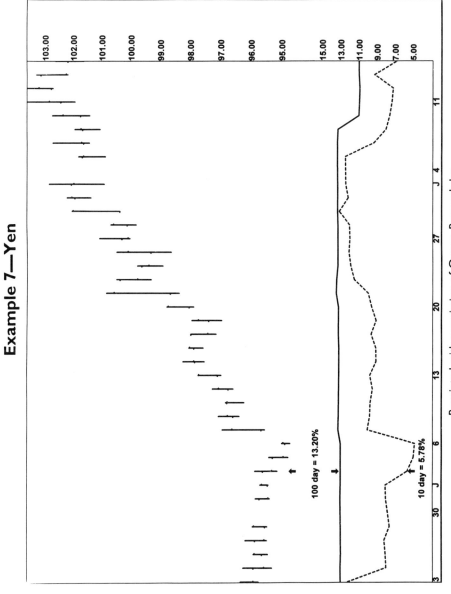

103.00
102.00
101.00
100.00
99.00
98.00
97.00
96.00
95.00
15.00
13.00
11.00
9.00
7.00
5.00

100 day = 13.20%

10 day = 5.78%

3   30   J   6   13   20   27   J 4   11

Reprinted with permission of Omega Research Inc.

GOLD AND SILVER INDEX:
JANUARY 1, 1992 TO NOVEMBER 1, 1994

The following examples are from the gold and silver index traded on the Philadelphia Stock Exchange.

Example #1. March 4, 1992, the 10-day historical volatility drops to 15.67 percent, while the 100-day reading is at 32.13 percent, warning us of a potential move. The market sells off sharply and drops more than 10 percent over the next three weeks.

Example 1—Gold and Silver

82.00
80.00
78.00
76.00
74.00
72.00
70.00
68.00
34.00
30.00
26.00
22.00
18.00
14.00

100 day = 32.13%

10 day = 15.67%

9   16   23

Reprinted with permission of Omega Research Inc.

Example #2. The next signal occurs on October 5, 1992. The 10-day H.V. reading reaches 13.85 percent, while the 100-day is at 28.16 percent. The market trades sideways for a few days before losing more than 20 percent of its value over the next seven weeks.

Example 2—Gold and Silver

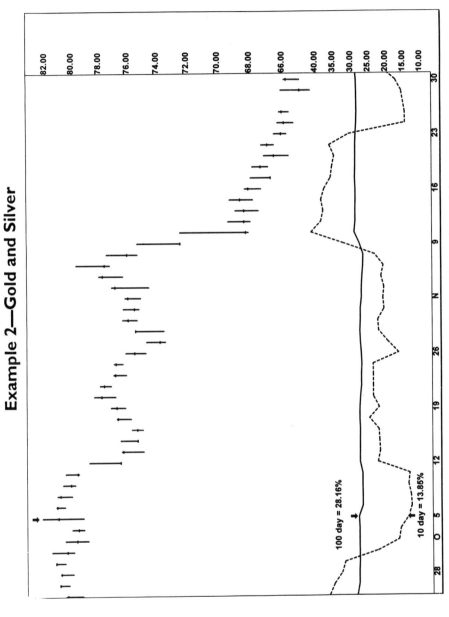

Reprinted with permission of Omega Research Inc.

Example #3. January 18, 1993, the 10-day reading reaches 10.92 percent, while the 100-day reading is at 25.54 percent. The signal occurs at the market's low, to the day, as the XAU explodes over 10 points over the next few weeks and approximately 60 points over the next six months.

Example 3—Gold and Silver

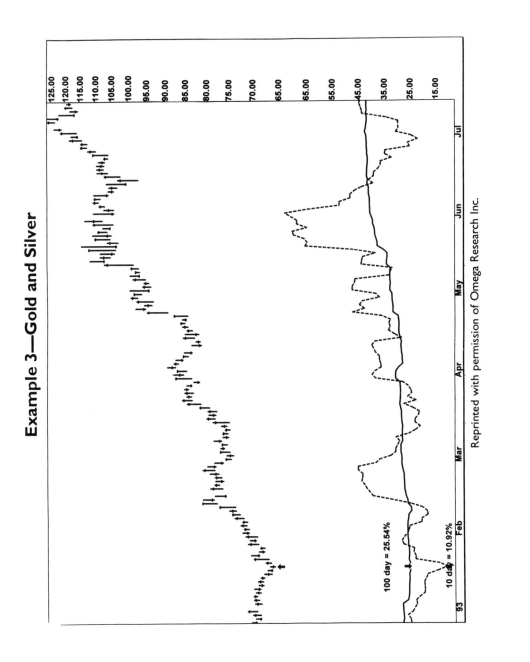

125.00		
120.00		
115.00		
110.00		
105.00		
100.00		
95.00		
90.00		
85.00		
80.00		
75.00		
70.00		
65.00		
65.00		
55.00		
45.00		
35.00		
25.00		
15.00		

100 day = 25.54%

10 day = 10.92%

93 Feb Mar Apr May Jun Jul

Reprinted with permission of Omega Research Inc.

Example #4. July 22, 1993, the 10-day reading is 20.93 percent, while the 100-day is at 41.91 percent. The market immediately advances more than 15 points over the next week.

Example 4—Gold and Silver

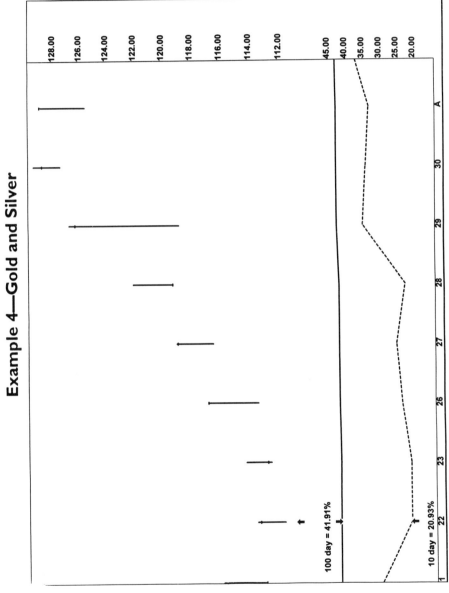

Reprinted with permission of Omega Research Inc.

Example #5. November 24, 1993, the 10-day H.V. reading reaches 19.30 percent, while the 100-day is at 40.42 percent. The market sells off for two days and reverses to the upside almost 20 points over the next three weeks.

Example 5—Gold and Silver

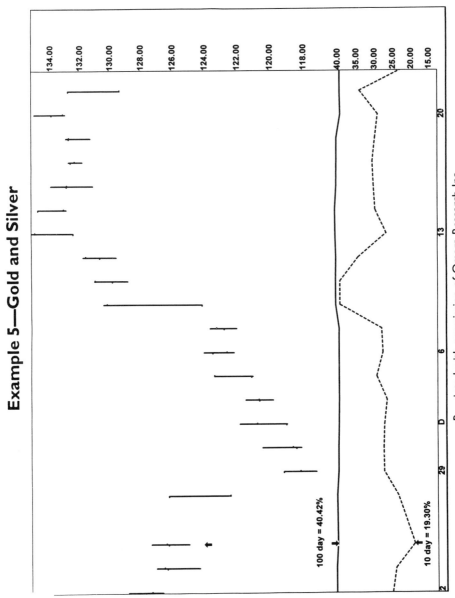

Reprinted with permission of Omega Research Inc.

Example #6. June 15, 1994, the signal misses the intermediate top by four days. The 10-day H.V. is at 16.49 percent, and the 100-day is at 34.43 percent. The index loses 10 percent of its value within three weeks.

Example 6—Gold and Silver

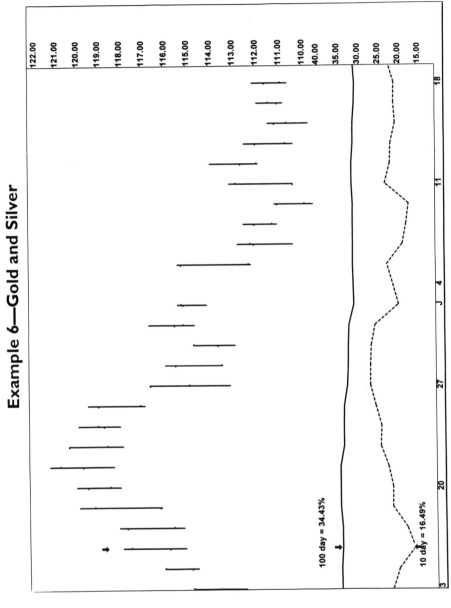

Reprinted with permission of Omega Research Inc.

Example #7. There was only one signal for 1994, and it was a good one.

On August 16, the 10-day reading is 13.33 percent, while the 100-day is 29.25 percent. The market climbs over 20 percent the next six weeks!

Example 7—Gold and Silver

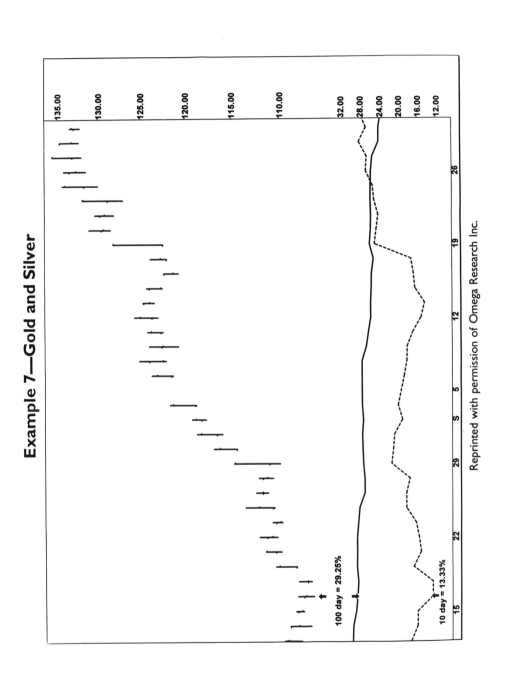

100 day = 29.25%

10 day = 13.33%

Reprinted with permission of Omega Research Inc.

SUMMARY

The Connors-Hayward Historical Volatility System has an uncanny ability to predict major moves. Unfortunately, it does not tell you in which direction the move will be. Therefore, the strategy you select will depend upon the strategies and indicators you are comfortable with. Some traders will trade options and buy both calls and puts on the signal date. Some traders will look for trend-line reversal or break-out patterns. Others will attempt to combine the signal with fundamental analysis. This is a personal choice.

Also, the 10-day and 100-day parameters used in this chapter are only one combination that works. Parameters are dependent upon the period of time one wishes to hold a position. Short-term traders should look at shorter time periods. Long-term traders should look at longer periods and at weekly and monthly parameters. Again, this is a personal choice.

When properly utilized, the Connors-Hayward Historical Volatility System is a powerful tool that helps the individual trader identify when explosive moves will occur.

Chapter Four

-
-
-
-
-

Undeniables™

*The whole idea is to somehow get an edge.
Sometimes it takes a little extra something
to get that edge, but you have to have it.*

Don Shula

Undeniables are a reversal pattern we use to trade index options. Currently (early 1995), there are over 35 indices available on which to trade index options. These include index groups such as consumer stocks, gambling stocks, healthcare stocks, computer stocks, and so on. (A complete list is in the appendix.) For example, if you are bullish on biotechnology stocks, you can buy calls on a basket of biotechnology companies.

We call the reversal pattern we use to identify turning points in stock indexes *undeniables*. When we first explained this trading strategy to a friend of ours who trades for one of the major brokerage houses, he said it was "undeniably" the greatest trading system ever. We assure you, this is not the greatest trading strategy ever, but it is pretty good. Since that time though, the term *undeniable* has stuck.

Undeniables have an uncanny ability to identify times when group indices reverse after an extended period of strength or weakness.

Here is how undeniables work:

1. Take the weekly chart of a stock index group.

2. Identify an intraweek price that has either made a six-week high or a six-week low.

3. For weeks that made lows, the close of that week *must* be above the open.

4. For weeks that made highs, the close of that week *must* be below the open.

5. For lows, a buy signal is triggered the next week if the index trades .25 points above the previous week's high.

6. For highs, a sell signal is triggered the next week if the index trades .25 points below the previous week's low.

7. Stops on buys are one tick below the reversal week low.

8. Stops on sells are one tick above the reversal week high.

9. If the following week does not trade above the high of the buy reversal week, there is no signal.

10. If the following week does not trade below the low of the sell reversal week, there is no signal.

We have found that this reversal pattern does a good job of identifying market reversals but that it does an even better job of identifying momentum coming out of a move.

Our experience has shown us that instead of using calls on buy signals and puts on sell signals, a much more profitable strategy is to be a seller of calls on sell signals and a seller of puts on buy reversals. Normally, this is a risky strategy; but unlike individual stocks, indexes cannot be bought out, and large gaps are rare.

The strategy we use to sell the options is as follows. If we have a sell reversal, we will take the high price of the reversal bar, round it off to its nearest strike price, and sell the calls (less aggressive investors will want to sell a bear call spread). For example, if the gold index (XAU) has a high of 118.50 and a low of 113.22 the week of its reversal bar, we will sell the next month's 120 calls (118.50 rounded off to the nearest strike price is 120).

If we have a buy reversal, we will take the low price of the reversal bar, round it off to its nearest strike price, and sell the puts. For example, if the software index has a low of 249.22 on its reversal bar, we will sell the following month's 250 puts (249.22 rounded off to the nearest strike price is 250).

Don't worry if this seems a bit complicated. We will walk you through five years of trades in the oil index, which will give you a better feel for the strategy.

The oil index (XOI) is traded on the AMEX. The index is made up of the 16 largest international oil companies traded on the NYSE. We have selected this index because during the five-year period November 24, 1989 to November 4, 1994, the index went through both a bull and bear market, yet our trading strategy was profitable over 70 percent of the time. These results are basically in line with the results achieved from other indices.

MARCH 30, 1990–NOVEMBER 2, 1990

Example #1. An undeniable pattern occurs on May 4, 1990. Notice that the week's low is the lowest low of the previous six weeks. Also notice that the weekly close is above the week's high. Finally, the following week trades .25 above the May 4 high, triggering a buy signal. Since the low of May 4 is 232.30, we will round it off to 230 and sell the following month's (June) 230 puts. We will cover our puts if the index trades below 232.30 at any time over the next four weeks. Unless we are stopped out of the position, we will hold our puts for the week and three additional weeks. This will allow ample time for our puts to decay in value.

Four weeks later (week of June 1) the index closes at 245.85, well above the 230 strike price we sold the puts. We can now comfortably close out our position for a healthy profit.

Example #2. Note that this is not a signal, even though the week of June 30 makes a six-week low and closes above its opening. The high of July 5, does not exceed the previous week's high.

Example #3. Not a trade. Even though the close is below the open, the week did not make a six-week high.

Examples 1–3—March 30, 1990–November 2, 1990

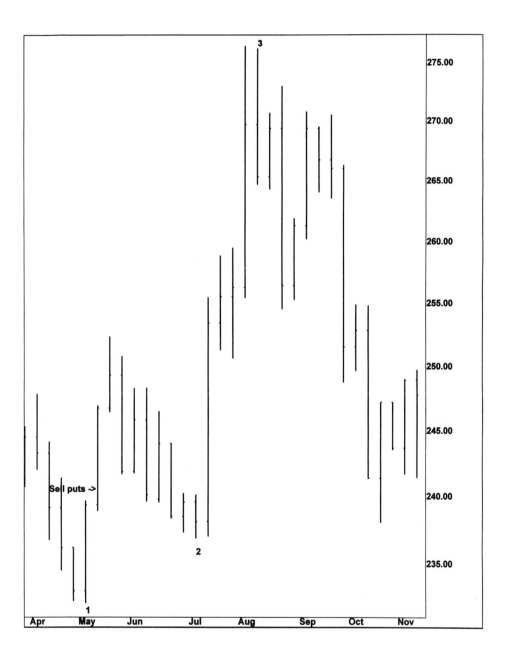

Reprinted with permission of Omega Research Inc.

NOVEMBER 9, 1990–OCTOBER 18, 1991

Example #1. January 18, 1991. The week makes a six-week low and closes above the open, giving us half our signal. The next week the market first trades lower and then reverses to trade .25 points higher than the previous week's high of 232.34. The low of 228.89 is rounded off to 230, and we will sell the February 230 puts. Our stop point is 228.38, one tick below the previous week's low. The market explodes to the upside two weeks later, and we can cover our puts for a nice profit.

Covering our puts with some time left is a personal choice. Usually the value of the options is so low it's not worth the risk to make a few extra dollars.

Example #2. July 12, 1991. Here is another signal. The index makes a six-week low and then reverses, with the week's close above the open. The next week a buy signal is triggered at 243.37, .25 points above the previous week's high. Since the low of the previous week was 234.28, we sell the August 235 puts, our stop being at 234.27. Four weeks later, the index is in the 250 range, well above the 235 strike price and we cover our short put position profitably.

Example #3. September 6, 1991. A sell reversal bar is indicated by a six-week high, accompanied by a close below the opening. The following week, the sell signal is triggered as the index trades more than .25 below the previous week's low of 251.38. The high of the undeniable bar is 255.52; therefore, the October 255 calls are sold. Four weeks later, the index is trading in the 250 range, and our calls are covered for a profit.

Notice how two weeks later (expiration week), the market explodes to 260. This is the reason we leave a small profit on the table by covering our short positions early.

Examples 1–3—November 9, 1990–October 18, 1991

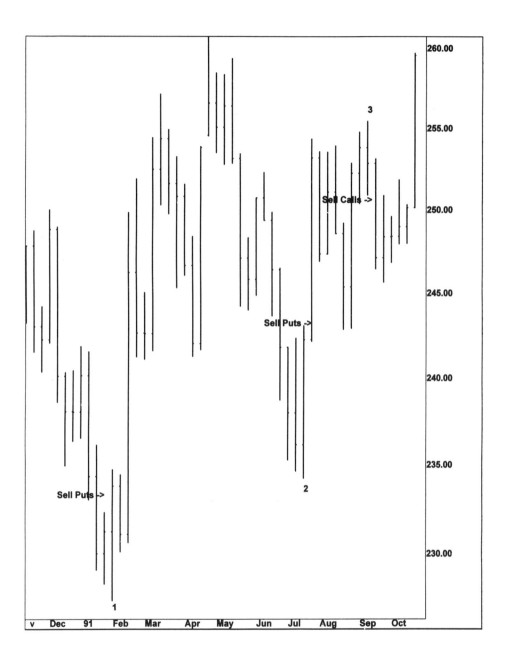

Reprinted with permission of Omega Research Inc.

OCTOBER 25, 1991–JULY 10, 1992

Example #1. An undeniable reversal is made the week of December 17, 1991. The following week, a signal is triggered on December 13 at 226.27 when prices exceed the previous week's high by .25 points. The low of the previous week was 218.04; therefore, we will sell the January 220 puts. The market rallies nicely for the next three weeks but reverses the fourth week. When you see a sell-off such as this, you may want to close your position a few days early. Even so, the fourth week closes at approximately our buy signal price, and we pick up four weeks of time decay in our options.

Example #2. The oil index reaches an intermediate-term high the week of January 24, 1992, and reverses. A sell signal is triggered the following week at 231.12, .25 points below the previous week's low. We will sell the March 230 calls.

Notice the week of February 13. The previous week made a six-week low and closed above its open. It then trades .25 points above the high of February 6, giving us a buy signal. We need to cover our short call position (for a small profit) and sell the March 220 puts.

Example #3. The first loss in over two years. After triggering a buy signal, the market reverses, trading under the low of 222.13 made the week of February 6. We cover our short put position for a small loss at 222.12, one tick under the reversal bar low (February 6).

Example #4. The week of March 17 has a reversal bar. Our buy signal is triggered the following week at 217.10. The low of the reversal bar is 211.46, so we sell the March 210 puts. The market moves sideways for a couple of weeks, and we then get stopped out as the market trades below 211.46 the week of April 3.

Example #5. This is a week that stops us out of our puts and then reverses. We get a new buy signal the next week at 216.92 and sell the May 210 puts. Over the next four weeks, the market rallies almost 20 points, leaving our puts virtually worthless.

Examples 1–5—October 25, 1991–July 10, 1992

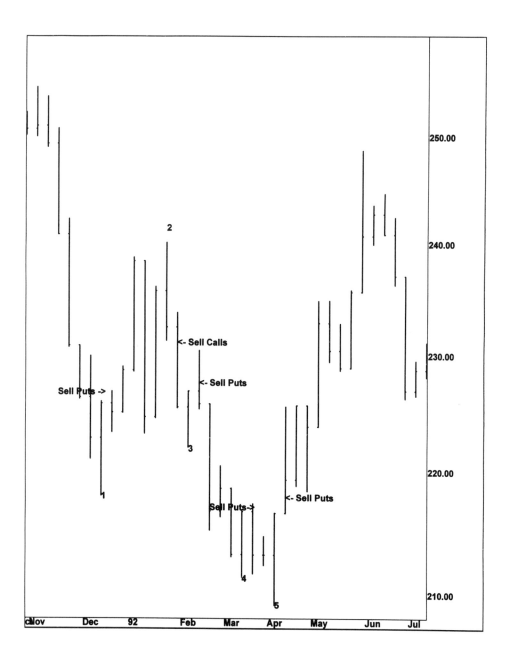

Reprinted with permission of Omega Research Inc.

JUNE 26, 1992–NOVEMBER 6, 1992

Example #1. The week of August 7 makes a six-week high of 240.46 and reverses. The following week trades .25 below the previous week's low of 234.71, triggering a sell signal. The September 240 calls are sold. We are immediately stopped out as the index trades above the August 7 high of 240.46.

Example #2. Another six-week high and a reversal. The index trades under the reversal bar low the next week, and a short sale is triggered. We again get stopped out the following week for a small loss.

Example #3. Again a six-week high and a close below the open. The following week triggers our sell signal, and we sell the October 245 calls. We cover the calls four weeks later for a nice profit.

Examples 1–3—June 26, 1992–November 6, 1992

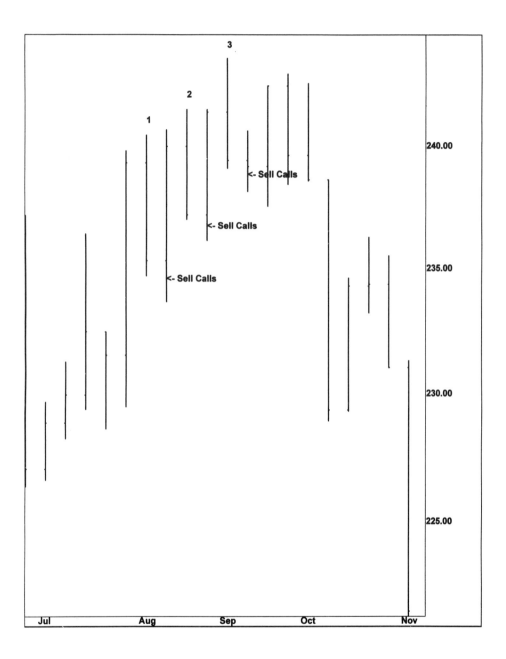

Reprinted with permission of Omega Research Inc.

NOVEMBER 13, 1992–NOVEMBER 26, 1993

Example #1. The index makes a new six-week high of 243.34 the week of February 12 and then closes below its open. The next week the market trades more than .25 points below the low made on February 12, and a sell signal is triggered. We will sell the March 245 calls with our stop at 243.35. The following week when the market trades at 243.35, we are stopped out.

Example #2. June 11. Another six-week high combined with a close below the opening is made. The next week a sell signal is triggered, and the July 265 calls we are short are comfortably profitable four weeks later.

Example #3. October 15. Again a six-week high and a reversal. We capture a nice profit for our short calls.

Examples 1–3—November 13, 1992–November 26, 1993

Reprinted with permission of Omega Research Inc.

DECEMBER 3, 1993–NOVEMBER 4, 1994

Example #1. A six-week high of 270.13 and a reversal. The sale of the March 270 calls made on the week of February 11 is again quite profitable four weeks later.

Example #2. A sharp sell-off is reversed the week of April 8. A buy signal is triggered the following week, and the short sale of the 240 puts are immediately profitable as the market rallies nicely.

Example #3. A six-week low and a reversal. The sale of the November 255 puts is quite profitable as the market moves higher over the next four weeks.

Examples 1–3—December 3, 1993–November 4, 1994

Reprinted with permission of Omega Research Inc.

SUMMARY

We thought it would be informative to take a five-year period of an index and look at it trade by trade.

The results are impressive:

13 profitable, 5 unprofitable = 72 percent correct

These results are in line with the results achieved in the other indices. Why do undeniables work? We believe it is a combination of four factors:

1. First, you have a six week high or low, which reverses itself during the week.

2. Second, you are waiting for the reversal to follow through the following week.

3. Third, you are selling options that are out of the money.

4. Fourth, you are using excellent money-management controls with your stops.

As with the reversal patterns shown in other chapters, you are identifying a market that has reached an overbought or oversold condition and climbing aboard for the ride as the reversal takes place.

Chapter Five

-
-
-
-
-

Connors-Hayward Advance-Decline Trading Pattern™

. . . in the affairs of men
There are tides, which taken
at the flood, lead on to fortune.

Shakespeare

The Connors-Hayward Advance-Decline Trading Pattern (CHADTP) is a proprietary indicator we use to identify short- and intermediate-term overbought and oversold conditions for the stock market and the S&P 500 futures market.

As we've mentioned, we are big proponents of trying to identify trend reversals. The biggest profits come from the times one can be a buyer at market bottoms and a seller at market tops. The CHADTP is an indicator that helps us identify those market reversals that lead to potentially substantial gains.

Construction of the CHADTP indicator is simple:

1. Add the past five day's advancing issues from the New York Stock Exchange.

2. Add the past five day's declining issues from the NYSE.

3. Subtract #2 from #1.

4. Divide by five.

Here are the two rules to trade CHADTP:

1. When the five-day reading is above +400, the market is over-bought; and when the five day reading is below -400, the market is oversold.

   Unfortunately, just because the indicator is -400 does not mean we can blindly buy the market, and just because the indicator is +400 does not mean we should be a seller of the market.

2. Whenever we get an overbought or oversold reading, we wait for a specific price reversal before entering. When the CHADTP number is +400 or more, we will sell the market only after the S&P 500 futures trade .10 points below the previous day's low. For example, if we get a reading of +422 and today's low is 453.80, we will take a sell signal only if the market trades at 453.70 or below tomorrow. If tomorrow the market low is 454.60, and the CHADTP is above 400, we will only sell if the market trades at 454.50 or below the next day, and so on.

   On the buy side, if today's CHADTP number is -400 or less, we will buy only after tomorrow's S&P trades .10 points above to-day's high, and so on.

The following examples will help you better understand the application of the rules, but first we need to mention the role the media plays in this trading strategy. As most people know, the newspapers are filled with negative quotes at market bottoms and positive quotes at market tops. You must be extra careful not to allow these quotes to dissuade you from taking the CHADTP signal. As the examples illustrate, the arguments made at these times by analysts and market prognosticators can be very persuasive, but you must avoid being influenced by them.

Example #1

1. On February 2, 1994, with the market trading at its all-time high, the CHADTP reaches +400.6, therefore warning us that the market is overbought. (Remember all CHADTP numbers are calculated after the close). The following day, if the March contract of the S&P 500 trades .10 points below the previous day's low of 479.65, a sell signal will be triggered.

2. Market euphoria is bubbling. The morning papers quote guru after guru proclaiming the market will blast through the 4000 level on its way to 4200. Even so, the market opens lower and begins to sell off. A CHADTP sell signal is triggered at 479.55, .10 points below the previous day's low.

3. Sometimes it helps to be a little lucky. One day after our sell signal is triggered, the Federal Reserve raises interest rates for the first time in 3 1/2 years. The market gets crushed (and so do the gurus) and closes down over 11 S&P points and over 87 Dow points.

4. Our research has found that the most consistent results using CHADTP occur over a five-to-seven-day period, trade date inclusive. (For further insights, see our analysis at the end of this chapter.) In this case, after six days, the market closes 9.65 S&P points below our sell short signal. (As of December 10, 1994, the S&P 500 has yet to trade higher than the February 2 high!)

This example, though informative, is not quite typical. It is rare to get such a major news event after a CHADTP signal is triggered. You will see in further examples, though, that gains made without news events can be just as significant.

Example 1—S&P Futures, March 1994

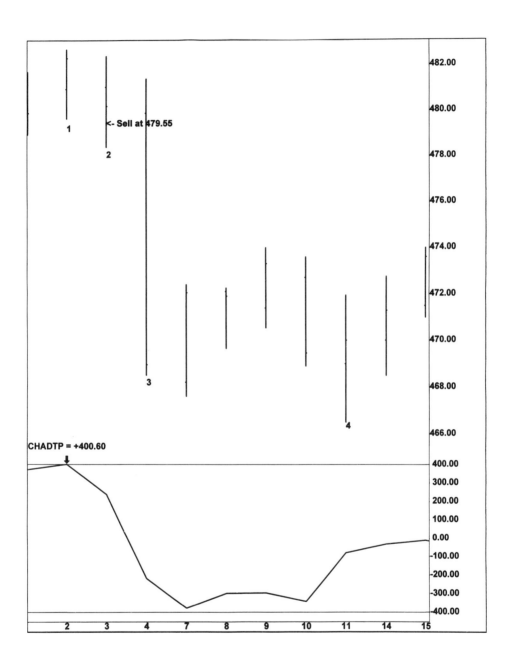

Reprinted with permission of Omega Research Inc.

Example #2

1. October 10, 1990—The CHADTP reaches -403.60, warning us that the market is oversold. We know that if the December futures contract of the S&P trades the next day .10 points above today's high of 309.30, a buy signal will be triggered.

2. October 11—The high is not .10 points higher than the previous day's high. We remain on the sidelines.

3. October 12—The high is again not .10 points above the previous day's high. Even though the market closes higher, we remain on the sidelines. We know we are getting close, though. *The Wall Street Journal* quotes a senior vice president of a money management firm as saying, "This is a scary time."

4. October 15. The market sells off sharply in the morning and then reverses. We get our buy signal at 304.35, which is triggered late in the day. We can now be fairly confident that the recent sell-off is over.

5. October 23. As mentioned, we have found that the best success occurs by staying in a position for five to seven trading days (trade day inclusive). In this example, over the six-day trading period, the market closes at 315.50, the S&P 500 has appreciated 11.15 points since our buy signal, and the Dow Jones Industrial Average has appreciated approximately 92 points over the same period of time. Futures traders realize a $5,000 plus profit per contract, and stock buyers have entered the market at an intermediate-term low.

Example 2—S&P 500 Futures, December 1990

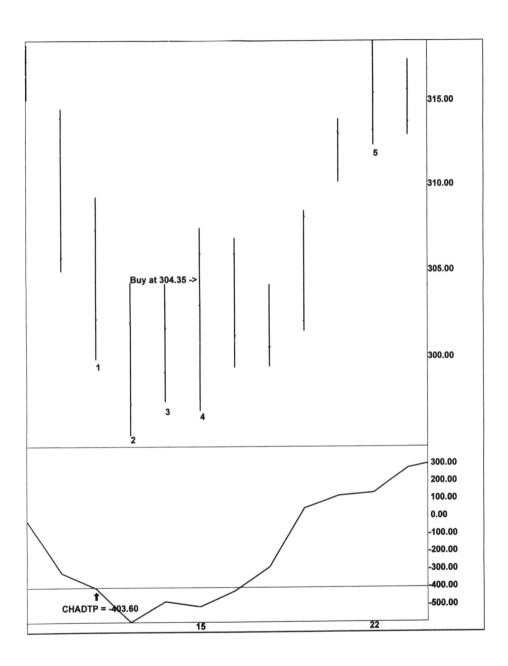

Reprinted with permission of Omega Research Inc.

Example# 3

1. April 8, 1992—Our CHADTP indicator reaches -472.80, warning us that the bottom is near. We will look to buy if the June S&P 500 the following day traded .10 points above the previous day's high of 397.70. To further warn us a bottom is near, the *New York Times* quotes a market analyst as saying, "Volume is so low that it tells you people are just depressed. That means we are likely to have a prolonged bottom to this market."

2. April 9—The morning's *New York Times* quotes the chief strategist of a major brokerage house as saying, "It doesn't appear as though the damage is finished."

   Shortly after the opening, the market blasts upward, triggering our buy signal at 397.80 and finishing the day up almost five S&P points and up 43.51 Dow points. (Now it appears the damage is finished).

3. April 16—The market is 19 S&P points higher and 144 Dow Points higher from our buy signal.

4. April 20—Seven trading days have passed, and it appears our move to the upside has been exhausted. A CHADTP sell signal was triggered the previous day.

   Though we are not big proponents of buying options, the potential gains after a CHADTP signal occurs are very large. On April 9, the day our signal was triggered, the OEX April 375 calls could be purchased at 2 5/8. They closed six days later at 16 1/8!

Example 3—S&P 500 Futures, June 1992

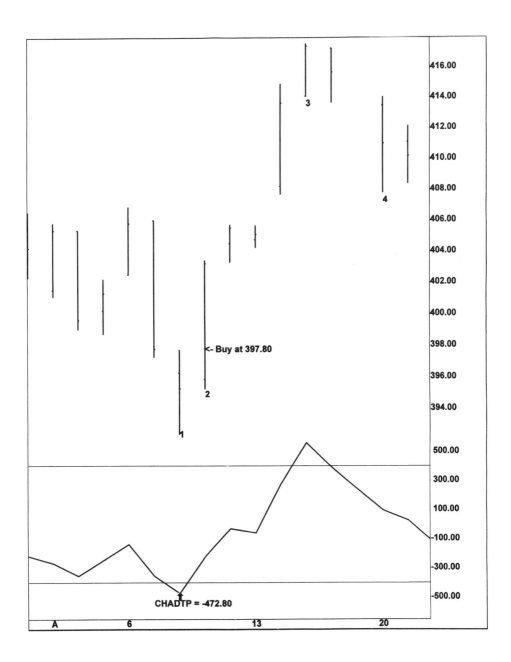

Reprinted with permission of Omega Research Inc.

Example #4

1. April 11, 1988—The CHADTP reaches +495.60, warning us of a market top.

2. April 12—The market doesn't trade .10 points below the previous day's low of 369.75. Therefore, a signal to go short is not given.

3. April 13—The *New York Times* quotes a money manager as saying, "The excess cash on the sidelines is beginning to feel the heat from this unexpected strength in equities." Even so, the market trades .10 points below the previous day's low, thereby giving us a sell signal.

4. April 20—Five trading days later, the S&P 500 is now 12.85 points lower, and the Dow is 100 points lower than the previous week.

Example 4—S&P 500 Futures, June 1988

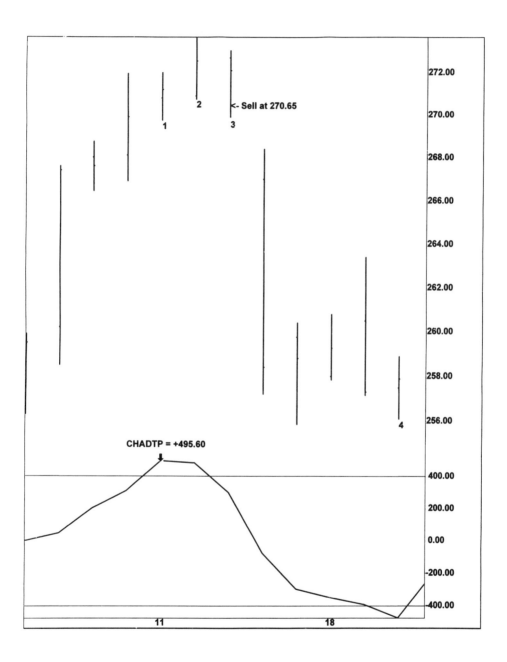

Reprinted with permission of Omega Research Inc.

Example #5

1. January 2, 1990—After the market advances sharply in late 1989, our CHADTP indicator gives an overbought reading of +405.80. *The Wall Street Journal* talks about the market's "cheery outlook."

2. January 3—The day's low is not .10 points lower than the previous day's low of 355.50. The *New York Times* talks about "positive seasonal factors."

3. January 4—The market trades .10 points below the previous day's low of 361.30, and a sell signal is rendered.

4. January 12—Seven trading days have passed, and the market's sell-off is significant. The S&P 500 is 20.25 points lower (more than $10,000 per S&P contract)!

By the way, a few days after our sell signal was rendered, a major newspaper quoted a money manager as saying that the market was "behaving pretty well." (Ouch!)

Option players made out well in this example. When the sell signal was triggered on January 4th, the January OEX 335 puts were trading at 4 7/8. They closed at 18 3/4 seven trading days later!

Example 5—S&P 500 Futures, March 1990

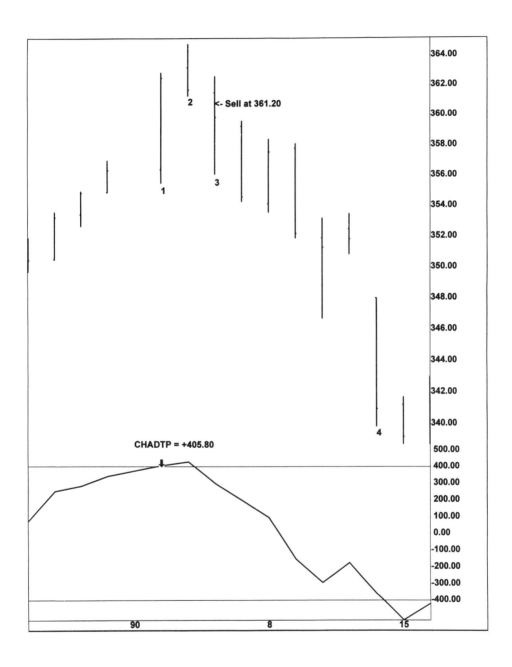

Reprinted with permission of Omega Research Inc.

SUMMARY

As you can see, the CHADTP does a good job of identifying short- and intermediate-term tops and bottoms. To prove the effectiveness of the CHADTP, we ran a study from January 1, 1988, to November 29, 1994. We used the same rules and exited on the close of the sixth trading day. During this period, the indicator was profitable 74 percent of the time! Also, due to the extreme nature of these moves, a number of option positions achieved returns in excess of 500 percent over a six-day period. (We recommend reviewing the trade summary that follows.)

There are many strategies one can employ using this indicator. On buy signals, one can buy stocks, buy calls, cover shorts, sell bull put spreads, buy the S&P 500 futures, and so on—all combined with various money-management strategies. On the sell side, you can use the opposite trading strategies.

The main use of this indicator is to keep you from becoming too wrapped up in the euphoria of a rising market and the gloom of a declining market. Remember, the biggest profits occur when you are buying while everyone else is selling, and selling while everyone else is buying.

CHADTP Performance Summary

chadtp S&P Index - CME-Daily 01/04/88 - 12/02/94

Performance Summary: All Trades

Total net profit	$49,525.00	Open position P/L	$ 0.00
Gross profit	$95,450.00	Gross loss	$-45,925.00
Total # of trades	53	**Percent profitable**	**74%**
Number winning trades	39	Number losing trades	14
Largest winning trade	$8,100.00	Largest losing trade	$8,250.00
Average winning trade	$2,447.44	Average losing trade	$-3,280.36
Ratio avg. win/avg loss	0.75	Avg trade (win & loss)	$934.43
Max consec. winners	7	Max consec. losers	3
Avg. # bars in winners	5	Avg # bars in losers	5
Max intraday drawdown	$-14,250.00		
Profit factor	2.08	Max # contracts held	1
Account size required	$14,250.00	Return on account	348%

Performance Summary: Long Trades

Total net profit	$44,725.00	Open position P/L	$ 0.00
Gross profit	$65,500.00	Gross loss	$-20,775.00
Total # of trades	33	**Percent profitable**	**76%**
Number winning trades	25	Number losing trades	8
Largest winning trade	$8,100.00	Largest losing trade	$-5,775.00
Average winning trade	$2,620.00	Average losing trade	$2,596.88
Ratio avg. win/avg loss	1.01	Avg trade (win & loss)	$1,355.30
Max consec. winners	14	Max consec. losers	2
Avg. # bars in winners	5	Avg # bars in losers	5
Max intraday drawdown	$-12,400.00		
Profit factor	3.15	Max # contracts held	1
Account size required	$12,400.00	Return on account	361%

Performance Summary: Short Trades

Total net profit	$4,800.00	Open position P/L	$ 0.00
Gross profit	$29,950.00	Gross loss	$-25,150.00
Total # of trades	20	**Percent profitable**	**70%**
Number winning trades	14	Number losing trades	6
Largest winning trade	$6,375.00	Largest losing trades	$-8,250.00
Average winning trade	$2,139.29	Average losing trade	$-4,191.67
Ratio avg. win/avg loss	0.51	Avg trade (win & loss)	$240.00
Max consec. winners	5	Max consec. losers	3
Avg # bars in winners	5	Avg. # bars in losers	5
Max intraday drawdown	$-15,425.00		
Profit factor	1.19	Max # contracts held	1
Account size required	$15,425.00	Return on account	31%

Reprinted with permission of Omega Research Inc.

CHADTP Trade Summary

chadtp S&P 500 Index—CME-Daily 01/04/88–12/02/94

Date	Time	Type	Cnts	Price	Signal Name	Entry P/L	Cumulative
03/29/88		Buy	1	261.05			
04/06/88		LExit	1	267.40		$ 3175.00	$ 3175.00
04/13/88		Sell	1	270.65			
04/20/88		SExit	1	257.90		$ 6375.00	$ 9550.00
04/21/88		Buy	1	259.00			
04/28/88		LExit	1	263.40		$ 2200.00	$11750.00
05/24/88		Buy	1	253.80			
06/01/88		LExit	1	266.85		$ 6525.00	$18275.00
06/07/88		Sell	1	264.50			
06/14/88		SExit	1	276.70		$−6100.00	$12175.00
06/15/88		Sell	1	275.00			
06/22/88		SExit	1	277.95		$−1475.00	$10700.00
08/12/88		Buy	1	263.90			
08/19/88		LExit	1	261.95		$ −975.00	$ 9725.00
11/18/88		Buy	1	266.90			
11/28/88		LExit	1	268.95		$ 1025.00	$10750.00
02/28/89		Buy	1	289.25			
03/07/89		LExit	1	294.90		$ 2825.00	$13575.00
07/12/89		Sell	1	331.00			
07/19/89		SExit	1	338.25		$−3625.00	$ 9950.00
10/18/89		Buy	1	345.40			
10/25/89		LExit	1	344.65		$ −375.00	$ 9575.00
10/31/89		Buy	1	339.70			
11/07/89		LExit	1	336.30		$−1700.00	$ 7875.00
12/21/89		Buy	1	348.60			
12/29/89		LExit	1	356.35		$ 3875.00	$11750.00
01/04/90		Sell	1	361.20			
01/11/90		SExit	1	351.85		$ 4675.00	$16425.00
01/16/90		Buy	1	341.80			
01/23/90		LExit	1	330.25		$−5775.00	$10650.00
01/25/90		Buy	1	334.00			
02/01/90		LExit	1	330.10		$−1950.00	$ 8700.00
04/26/90		Buy	1	335.05			

chadtp S&P 500 Index—CME-Daily 01/04/88–12/02/94

Date	Time	Type	Cnts	Price	Signal Name	Entry P/L	Cumulative
05/03/90		LExit	1	337.15		$ 1050.00	$ 9750.00
07/25/90		Buy	1	358.45			
08/01/90		LExit	1	357.45		$ −500.00	$ 9250.00
08/08/90		Buy	1	341.10			
08/15/90		LExit	1	341.65		$ 275.00	$ 9525.00
08/24/90		Buy	1	313.20			
08/31/90		LExit	1	322.55		$ 4675.00	$14200.00
09/26/90		Buy	1	311.65			
10/03/90		LExit	1	313.70		$ 1025.00	$15225.00
10/15/90		Buy	1	304.35			
10/22/90		LExit	1	315.50		$ 5575.00	$20800.00
11/15/90		Sell	1	318.30			
11/23/90		SExit	1	315.50		$ 1400.00	$22200.00
12/07/90		Sell	1	329.00			
12/14/90		SExit	1	327.20		$ 900.00	$23100.00
01/29/91		Sell	1	336.30			
02/05/91		SExit	1	352.80		$−8250.00	$14850.00
02/13/91		Sell	1	366.00			
02/21/91		SExit	1	365.90		$ 50.00	$14900.00
06/04/91		Sell	1	387.50			
06/11/91		SExit	1	382.10		$ 2700.00	$17600.00
06/26/91		Buy	1	375.50			
07/03/91		LExit	1	376.00		$ 250.00	$17850.00
08/27/91		Sell	1	393.50			
09/04/91		SExit	1	391.20		$ 1150.00	$19000.00
11/26/91		Buy	1	378.20			
12/04/91		LExit	1	380.55		$ 1175.00	$20175.00
01/02/92		Sell	1	414.20			
01/09/92		SExit	1	418.95		$−2375.00	$17800.00
04/09/92		Buy	1	397.80			
04/16/92		LExit	1	414.00		$ 8100.00	$25900.00
04/16/92		Sell	1	414.00			
04/24/92		SExit	1	408.80		$ 2600.00	$28500.00
06/23/92		Buy	1	404.50			

chadtp S&P 500 Index—CME-Daily   01/04/88–12/02/94

Date	Time	Type	Cnts	Price	Signal Name	Entry P/L	Cumulative
06/30/92		LExit	1	409.50		$ 2500.00	$31000.00
08/26/92		Buy	1	412.00			
09/02/92		LExit	1	418.10		$ 3050.00	$34050.00
02/05/93		Sell	1	448.00			
02/12/93		SExit	1	444.70		$ 1650.00	$35700.00
03/04/93		Sell	1	447.75			
03/11/93		SExit	1	454.40		$–3325.00	$32375.00
11/08/93		Buy	1	460.00			
11/15/93		LExit	1	464.30		$ 2150.00	$34525.00
11/23/93		Buy	1	461.70			
12/01/93		LExit	1	462.90		$ 600.00	$35125.00
02/03/94		Sell	1	479.55			
02/10/94		SExit	1	469.45		$ 5050.00	$40175.00
04/05/94		Buy	1	443.00			
04/12/94		LExit	1	448.00		$ 2500.00	$42675.00
04/21/94		Buy	1	445.00			
04/29/94		LExit	1	447.15		$ 1075.00	$43750.00
04/29/94		Sell	1	447.15			
05/06/94		SExit	1	446.60		$ 275.00	$44025.00
05/10/94		Buy	1	446.60			
05/17/94		LExit	1	450.65		$ 2025.00	$46050.00
06/23/94		Buy	1	455.50			
06/30/94		LExit	1	445.05		$–5225.00	$40825.00
08/04/94		Sell	1	459.80			
08/11/94		SExit	1	458.40		$ 700.00	$41525.00
08/30/94		Sell	1	474.25			
09/07/94		SExit	1	470.65		$ 1800.00	$43325.00
09/27/94		Buy	1	463.60			
10/04/94		LExit	1	455.05		$–4275.00	$39050.00
10/06/94		Buy	1	455.85			
10/13/94		LExit	1	469.15		$ 6650.00	$45700.00
10/14/94		Sell	1	467.00			
10/21/94		SExit	1	465.75		$ 625.00	$46325.00
10/26/94		Buy	1	463.50			

chadtp S&P 500 Index—CME-Daily   01/04/88–12/02/94

Date	Time	Type	Cnts	Price	Signal Name	Entry P/L	Cumulative
11/02/94		LExit	1	466.85		$ 1675.00	$48000.00
11/08/94		Buy	1	465.00			
11/15/94		LExit	1	465.65		$ 325.00	$48325.00
11/25/94		Buy	1	451.50			
12/02/94		LExit	1	453.90		$ 1200.00	$49525.00

Reprinted with permission of Omega Research Inc.

Chapter Six

-
-
-
-
-

New Markets,
New Indicators

*We keep moving forward, opening doors,
and doing new things, because we're curious
and curiosity keeps leading us down new paths.*

Walt Disney

NDX-SPX

The NDX-SPX indicator is used to predict future stock market movement. We have observed and our tests have proven that the NASDAQ 100 Index tends to lead the S&P 500 Index both to the upside and to the downside.

Before we go further, let us briefly describe the makeup of each index. The S&P 500 Index (SPX) is comprised of 500 major stocks representing a broad array of industries. The NASDAQ 100 Index (NDX) is made up of the largest 100 O.T.C. Stocks. The index is overweighed with growth stocks and so-called "momentum stocks." Companies such as Microsoft, Intel, Amgen, and Cisco Systems make this index more volatile than the S&P 500.

The stocks in the NASDAQ 100 tend to attract the "fast money." We have observed that the NASDAQ 100 gains in value ahead of the other market indices and loses value ahead of the other indices.

To prove our observation, we ran a study from January 1, 1991, to November 29, 1994. The study rules were as follows:

1. Take today's closing change of the NASDAQ 100 and the S&P 500.

2. If the NASDAQ 100 Index performance is stronger than the S&P 500 cash index, buy the S&P futures on the opening the next day.

3. Sell your position and reverse on the day following the NASDAQ 100 Index underperforming the S&P 500 cash index.

For example, if the NASDAQ is up 3.61 points today, and the S&P 500 cash market is up 2.41, you will buy the S&P 500 futures on the opening the next day and stay long until the S&P 500 cash outperforms the NASDAQ 100. The day after the S&P 500 index is stronger than the NASDAQ 100, you will sell the market (S&P 500 futures) on the opening and remain short until the NASDAQ 100 outperforms the S&P 500.

NDX-SPX Performance Summary

NDX-SPX S&P 500 Index - CME-Daily 01/02/91 - 11/30/94

Performance Summary: All Trades

Total net profit	**$133,725.00**	Open position P/L	$-500.00
Gross profit	$411,975.00	Gross loss	$-278,250.00
Total # of trades	440	Percent profitable	56%
Number winning trades	248	Number losing trades	192
Largest winning trade	$9,750.00	Largest losing trade	$-8,225.00
Average winning trade	$1,661.19	Average losing trade	$-1,449.22
Ratio avg win/avg loss	1.15	Avg trade (win & loss)	$303.92
Max consec. winners	12	Max consec. losers	5
Avg. # bars in winners	2	Avg. # bars in losers	2
Max intraday drawdown	$-20,250.00		
Profit factor	1.48	Max # contracts held	1
Account size required	$20,250.00	Return on account	660%

Performance Summary: Long Trades

Total net profit	$99,400.00	Open position P/L	$-500.00
Gross profit	$225,725.00	Gross loss	$-126,325.00
Total # of trades	220	Percent profitable	59%
Number winning trades	129	Number losing trades	91
Largest winning trade	$9,200.00	Largest losing trade	$-8,125.00
Average winning trade	$1,749.81	Average losing trade	$-1,388.19
Ratio avg. win/avg loss	1.26	Avg trade (win & loss)	$451.82
Max consec. winners	9	Max consec. losers	7
Avg # bars in winners	2	Avg # bars in losers	2
Max intraday drawdown	$-13,925.00		
Profit factor	1.79	Max # contracts held	1
Account size required	$13,925.00	Return on account	714%

Performance Summary: Short Trades

Total net profit	34,325.00	Open position P/L	$ 0.00
Gross profit	$186,250.00	Gross loss	$-151,925.00
Total # of trades	220	Percent profitable	54%
Number winning trades	119	Number losing trades	101
Largest winning trade	$9,750.00	Largest losing trade	$-8,225.00
Average winning trade	$1,565.13	Average losing trade	$-1,504.21
Ratio avg win/avg loss	1.04	Avg trade (win & loss)	$156.02
Max consec. winners	8	Max consec. losers	7
Avg # bars in winners	2	Avg. # bars in losers	2
Max intraday drawdown	$-12,500.00		
Profit factor	1.23	Max # contracts held	1
Account size required	$12,500.00	Return on account	275%

Reprinted with permission of Omega Research Inc.

NDX-SPX *DWI X S-Daily 01/02/91 - 11/30/94

Performance Summary: All Trades

Total net profit*	**2031.89**	Open position P/L	30.28
Gross profit	6,672.31	Gross loss	-4,640.42
Total # of trades	440	Percent profitable	55%
Number winning trades	241	Number losing trades	199
Largest winning trade	187.42	Largest losing trade	-157.43
Average winning trade	27.69	Average losing trade	-23.32
Ratio avg. win/avg loss	1.19	Avg trade (win & loss)	4.62
Max consec. winners	10	Max consec. losers	4
Avg. # bars in winners	2	Avg. # bars in losers	2
Max intraday drawdown	-325.00		
Profit facotr	1.44	Max # contracts held	1
Account size required	325.00	Return on account	625%

Performance Summary: Long Trades

Total net profit	1,583.29	Open position P/L	30.28
Gross profit	3,616.64	Gross loss	-2,033.35
Total # of trades	220	Percent profitable	60%
Number winning trades	133	Number losing trades	87
Largest winning trade	142.22	Largest losing trade	-148.37
Average winning trade	27.19	Average losing trade	-23.37
Ratio avg. win/avg loss	1.16	Avg trade (win & loss)	7.20
Max consec. winners	10	Max consec. losers	4
Avg. # bars in winners	2	Avg. # bars in losers	2
Max intraday drawdown	-244.26		
Profit factor	1.78	Max # contracts held	1
Account size required	244.26	Return on account	648%

Performance Summary: Short Trades

Total net profit	448.60	Open position P/L	0.00
Gross profit	3,055.67	Gross loss	-2,607.07
Total # of trades	220	Percent profitable	49%
Number winning trades	108	Number losing trades	112
Largest winning trade	187.42	Largest losing trade	-157.43
Average winning trade	28.29	Average losing trade	-23.28
Ratio avg. win/avg loss	1.22	Avg trade (win & loss)	2.04
Max consec. winners	7	Max consec. losers	9
Avg. # bars in winners	2	Avg. # bars in losers	2
Max intraday drawdown	-339.60		
Profit factor	1.17	Max # contracts held	1
Account size required	339.60	Return on account	132%

*Total Dow points.

Reprinted with permission of Omega Research Inc.

As you can see, the results are somewhat amazing. With this mechanical system, you gained over 260 S&P future points while a buy-and-hold strategy gained 131 points over the same period. The results for the Dow Jones Industrial Average are just as startling. The program gained 2031 Dow points versus 1173 points for the buy-and-hold strategy. Even more significant is that this mechanical system was profitable on the short side during a major bull market!

Another exciting aspect of this indicator is that it can be combined with other indicators for even stronger results. For example, by combining NDX-SPX with other short-term indicators, we have been able to create a number of systems that have tested over 80 percent correct!

Will the NASDAQ 100 continue to front-run the other averages in the future? We don't know. For the time being though, one should keep an eye out for this phenomena and consider implementing an appropriate strategy to exploit it.

VIX

The CBOE OEX Volatility Index (VIX) is a new indicator introduced in 1993. VIX reflects a market consensus estimate of future volatility, based on "at the money" quotes of the OEX index options. Throughout 1993 and 1994, the VIX traded mostly in the 11–12.5 range. Periods of short-term price decline are accompanied by higher VIX readings (more volatility); whereas, periods of short-term price appreciation are accompanied by lower VIX readings (less volatility). When readings become excessively high or excessively low, short-term market reversals tend to occur. These reversals are opportunities that S&P day traders can exploit.

Here are the rules of our VIX day trading program:

1. The VIX must close above 15 or below 11 for us to have a signal. This has historically occurred less than 30 percent of the time. All readings in between are ignored.

2. On readings above 15, the following trading day's opening must not gap higher on the opening. On the readings below 11, the

following trading day's opening must not gap lower on the opening.

3. The day following a closing VIX reading of 15 or more, a buy stop is placed .50 points above the previous day's high. The day following a closing VIX reading of 11 or less, a sell stop is placed .50 points below the previous day's low.

4. If the day following the signal day is an inside day (high is lower than the previous day's high and the low is higher than the previous day's low), the signal will be carried into the next trading day.

5. A stop is placed 200 points below your fill on buy days and 200 points above your fill on sell days.

6. Use a trailing stop to lock into profits or cover market on close.

The following are two examples to help clarify the rules.

Example #1. On November 7, 1994, the VIX has a closing reading of 16.36, giving us a potential signal. The next morning, the market does not gap higher, so we place a buy stop at 465.40, .50 points above the previous day's high. Upon being filled, a protective sell stop is placed at 463.40, 200 points under our buy stop. The market trades higher throughout the day and closes at 466.95, 1.55 points above our buy point.

Example I

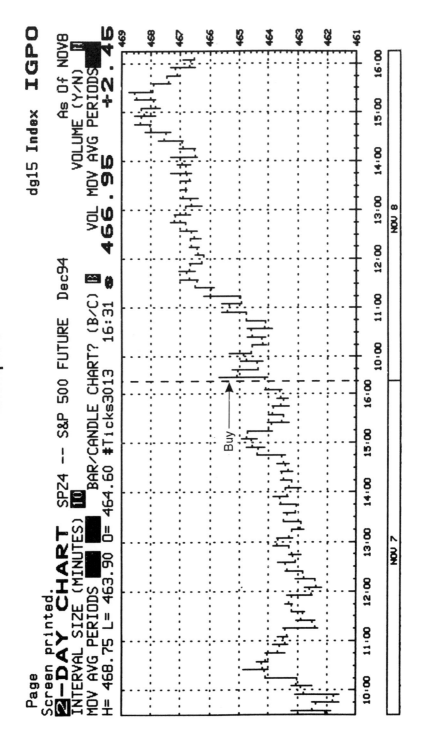

Reprinted with permission of Bloomberg L.P.

Example #2. On November 11, 1994, the VIX closes at 16.92, triggering a potential buy signal for the next trading day. On November 14, the market does not gap higher, and a buy stop is placed at 465.75. Upon being filled, a protective sell stop is placed at 463.75. The market trends higher most of the day and closes at 467.10, 135 points above our buy point.

The CBOE introduced the VIX indicator in early 1993. Since that time (through November 20, 1994), there have been 99 occasions the VIX has traded above 15 or below 11. Of those 99 occasions, there have been 24 trades based on the previous rules. The results have been promising: 14 profits; 10 losses; total profits closing the position M.O.C. is $10,875 per contract (includes $50 slippage and commission per trade).

Because this indicator is so new, one should be careful trading this strategy. Up until now though, the results have been extremely promising. We believe further research will prove the VIX an excellent indicator of predicting market reversals.

Example 2

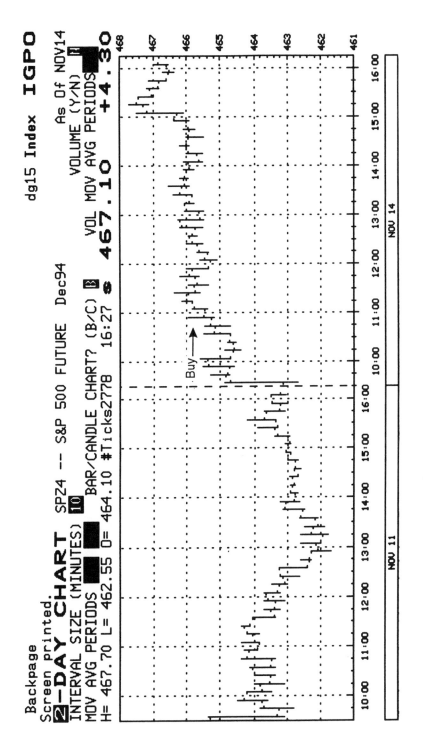

Reprinted with permission of Bloomberg L.P.

GLOBEX

In February 1990, we were fortunate enough to meet Michael Marcus. For those of you who don't recognize the name, Michael was the first trader to be featured in *Market Wizards*. All Michael did to deserve this honor was turn $30,000 into $80 million over a decade's time.

At the time we met him, Michael felt that one could no longer expect to dominate the markets as he had by trend-trading the large markets. He felt the greater opportunities lay in trading a different style in the less popular and newer markets. Michael's prediction has proven prophetic. Over the past five years, most of the larger trend-following funds have achieved dismal results. The individuals using innovative techniques have produced the better returns in the 90s.

We have discovered that the Globex and night trading markets fit Michael Marcus's criteria. As this is being written, these markets are basically undiscovered, and inefficiencies exist almost nightly.

We will share with you an example of these inefficiencies and how we trade these inefficiencies and will leave you with two profitable trading systems to trade the after-market sessions.

One evening, we were trading our Globex S&P Fair Value Program (explained later in the chapter). In our attempt to identify any large orders in the system, we learned there was an order to buy 300 contracts of the S&P 500 at 454.50 (300 contracts is currently a very large order for Globex). The next morning, while the Globex market was still open, there was a very bearish economic report. The bond market instantly sold off 3/4 of a point, yet the Globex market was holding at 454.50, virtually unchanged. We realized the order to buy the 300 contracts at 454.50 was still in the system. We, along with a handful of alert traders, called the Globex desk and immediately hit the bid at 454.50. Within seconds, the final contracts traded at 454.50, and the market immediately sank 150 points, where we covered our short position. We made 150 points in less than two minutes. This could only happen on the Globex system. If this had occurred during the day session, the 300 lot would have been taken out within seconds of the news.

We can give example after example of the inefficiencies we have seen in the Globex markets. For those willing to spend the time, the currency markets, due to their lack of liquidity, offer the astute speculator opportunities galore to scalp from. By watching the cash market simultaneously with the futures market, an alert trader can effectively scalp this market on a nightly basis.

Our most effective use of the evening markets, though, is not to scalp the Globex markets, but to trade pricing programs we have developed. The following are two of these programs.

Globex S&P Fair Value Program

This is one of our most consistent trading methods. This program combines the inefficient pricing of the S&P market caused by M.O.C. (Market On Close) orders with Globex trading.

Here's how it works:

1. Each day you need to find out what the fair value difference of the S&P futures is to the S&P cash market. This information can be obtained from your broker, CNBC, or possibly your computer program.

2. At 4:03 P.M. (EST), take the closing cash value of the S&P 500 cash market and add the fair value to the cash number. The reason you wait until 4:03 is because it takes a few minutes for market on close orders to be computed.

3. Add an additional .50 points to the number derived in step 2.

4. Place a sell stop on the S&P 500 futures at the price obtained from step 3.

5. If filled, cover your short at fair value (your fill minus 50 points) during Globex trading. You have over 16 hours to get filled.

6. Make sure you do not carry the position into economic news the next morning at 8:30 A.M. (EST). Close the position before the news! Remember this is a scalping method, and one economic report will wipe out many weeks of profits.

A note to the above rules. If at 4:03 (EST) the S&P futures market is trading at a substantial amount over fair value plus .50, it means the market is strong. You may be able to get a higher fill selling M.O.C.

Example

Step 1: On Friday, October 14, 1994, the fair value for the S&P 500 futures market was 1.42 points above the cash market.

Step 2: At 4:03 P.M. (EST), the cash market settled at 469.10. Add 1.42 to 469.10, which gives us a fair value number of 470.52, which we round off to 470.50.

Step 3: Adding .50 points to 470.50 gives us 471.00.

Step 4: A sell order is placed at 471.00 for the remaining few minutes of trading. We are filled at 471.00 a few minutes later, and the market closed at 471.25. (Sometimes we sell at the top; in this case the market kept going).

Step 5: On Sunday evening, we place a buy order at fair value (470.50). The market opens 471.00 and proceeds to sell off, giving us our fill at 470.50 for a 50-point profit (the market eventually reached a low of 469.60).

We do not trade this method from the long side. We would much rather be short the market in the evening. We believe market traders fear the worst overnight and would prefer to buy the market the next day when any and all news can be properly assimilated. That is why when the market trades above fair value it has an overwhelming tendency to correct itself on the Globex market. This method has worked extremely well during a period that we would classify as a bull market (1993–1994). We feel it will be even more profitable during a bear market.

Bond Market Evening Session Price Persistency Program

This method is employed trading the 30-year Treasury bond market in the day and evening sessions.

Here is how it works:

1. There must be a major economic report tomorrow morning to consider this trade. Major economic reports are defined as the unemployment numbers, C.P.I., P.P.I., trade deficit reports, or any other news event that could significantly affect the bond market.

2. If bonds are trading within three ticks of the day session lows in the final five minutes of trading, sell the bonds M.O.C.

3. Cover your short position in the evening at least five ticks lower or M.O.C. We do not like to carry our position overnight. Stops should be five ticks above your day session fill.

If bonds close near their low of the day ahead of economic news, it means traders are concerned about the report. This concern spills over into the evening sessions, causing further weakness. This method will give you a few trades per month, and the high percentage of profitability makes it a worthwhile venture.

The night markets are not for investors. They are for short-term traders who wish to scalp the markets for a few hundred dollars per contract. In time, as they become more popular, the inefficiencies we described will occur less often. We believe, though, that the S&P 500 and bond market trading methods we described will remain intact for many years.

NDX-SPX Trade Summary

NDX–SPX S&P 500 Index—CME–Daily 01/02/91–11/30/94

Date	Time	Type	Cnts	Price	Signal Name	Entry P/L	Cumulative
01/04/91		Buy	1	324.80			
01/14/91		LExit	1	313.00		$–5900.00	$ 5900.00
01/14/91		Sell	1	313.00			
01/15/91		SExit	1	314.10		$ –550.00	$ –6450.00
01/15/91		Buy	1	314.10			
01/18/91		LExit	1	330.25		$ 8075.00	$ 1625.00
01/18/91		Sell	1	330.25			
01/22/91		SExit	1	332.10		$ –925.00	$ 700.00
01/22/91		Buy	1	332.10			
01/25/91		LExit	1	336.50		$ 2200.00	$ 2900.00
01/25/91		Sell	1	336.50			
01/29/91		SExit	1	336.30		$ 100.00	$ 3000.00
01/29/91		Buy	1	336.30			
01/31/91		LExit	1	341.80		$ 2750.00	$ 5750.00
01/31/91		Sell	1	341.80			
02/01/91		SExit	1	343.00		$ –600.00	$ 5150.00
02/01/91		Buy	1	343.00			
02/05/91		LExit	1	348.75		$ 2875.00	$ 8025.00
02/05/91		Sell	1	348.75			
02/06/91		SExit	1	351.80		$–1525.00	$ 6500.00
02/06/91		Buy	1	351.80			
02/07/91		LExit	1	360.50		$ 4350.00	$ 10850.00
02/07/91		Sell	1	360.50			
02/13/91		SExit	1	366.50		$–3000.00	$ 7850.00
02/13/91		Buy	1	366.50			
02/14/91		LExit	1	370.00		$ 1750.00	$ 9600.00
02/14/91		Sell	1	370.00			
02/15/91		SExit	1	366.10		$ 1950.00	$ 11550.00
02/15/91		Buy	1	366.10			
02/19/91		LExit	1	369.00		$ 1450.00	$ 13000.00
02/19/91		Sell	1	369.00			
02/20/91		SExit	1	368.50		$ 250.00	$ 13250.00
02/20/91		Buy	1	368.50			

NDX–SPX S&P 500 Index—CME–Daily 01/02/91–11/30/94

Date	Time	Type	Cnts	Price	Signal Name	Entry P/L	Cumulative
02/22/91		LExit	1	364.60		$–1950.00	$ 11300.00
02/22/91		Sell	1	364.60			
02/25/91		SExit	1	371.00		$–3200.00	$ 8100.00
02/25/91		Buy	1	371.00			
02/26/91		LExit	1	366.00		$–2500.00	$ 5600.00
02/26/91		Sell	1	366.00			
02/27/91		SExit	1	364.50		$ 750.00	$ 6350.00
02/27/91		Buy	1	364.50			
02/28/91		LExit	1	370.30		$ 2900.00	$ 9250.00
02/28/91		Sell	1	370.30			
03/01/91		SExit	1	363.40		$ 3450.00	$ 12700.00
03/01/91		Buy	1	363.40			
03/04/91		LExit	1	372.25		$ 4425.00	$ 17125.00
03/04/91		Sell	1	372.25			
03/05/91		SExit	1	370.60		$ 825.00	$ 17950.00
03/05/91		Buy	1	370.60			
03/11/91		LExit	1	379.40		$ 4400.00	$ 22350.00
03/11/91		Sell	1	379.40			
03/14/91		SExit	1	379.40		$ 0.00	$ 22350.00
03/14/91		Buy	1	379.40			
03/15/91		LExit	1	376.80		$–1300.00	$ 21050.00
03/15/91		Sell	1	376.80			
03/19/91		SExit	1	372.00		$ 2400.00	$ 23450.00
03/19/91		Buy	1	372.00			
03/22/91		LExit	1	369.20		$–1400.00	$ 22050.00
03/22/91		Sell	1	369.20			
03/26/91		SExit	1	372.30		$–1550.00	$ 20500.00
03/26/91		Buy	1	372.30			
04/01/91		LExit	1	376.40		$ 2050.00	$ 22550.00
04/01/91		Sell	1	376.40			
04/02/91		SExit	1	374.25		$ 1075.00	$ 23625.00
04/02/91		Buy	1	374.25			
04/09/91		LExit	1	380.40		$ 3075.00	$ 26700.00
04/09/91		Sell	1	380.40			

NDX–SPX S&P 500 Index—CME–Daily 01/02/91–11/30/94

Date	Time	Type	Cnts	Price	Signal Name	Entry P/L	Cumulative
04/10/91		SExit	1	375.80		$ 2300.00	$ 29000.00
04/10/91		Buy	1	375.80			
04/11/91		LExit	1	377.00		$ 600.00	$ 29600.00
04/11/91		Sell	1	377.00			
04/12/91		SExit	1	382.00		$–2500.00	$ 27100.00
04/12/91		Buy	1	382.00			
04/15/91		LExit	1	383.00		$ 500.00	$ 27600.00
04/15/91		Sell	1	383.00			
04/22/91		SExit	1	385.75		$–1375.00	$ 26225.00
04/22/91		Buy	1	385.75			
04/29/91		LExit	1	380.90		$–2425.00	$ 23800.00
04/29/91		Sell	1	380.90			
04/30/91		SExit	1	375.25		$ 2825.00	$ 26625.00
04/30/91		Buy	1	375.25			
05/01/91		LExit	1	376.25		$ 500.00	$ 27125.00
05/01/91		Sell	1	376.25			
05/03/91		SExit	1	381.40		$–2575.00	$ 24550.00
05/03/91		Buy	1	381.40			
05/09/91		LExit	1	380.20		$ –600.00	$ 23950.00
05/09/91		Sell	1	380.20			
05/13/91		SExit	1	377.80		$ 1200.00	$ 25150.00
05/13/91		Buy	1	377.80			
05/14/91		LExit	1	376.25		$ –775.00	$ 24375.00
05/14/91		Sell	1	376.25			
05/15/91		SExit	1	372.90		$ 1675.00	$ 26050.00
05/15/91		Buy	1	372.90			
05/16/91		LExit	1	371.20		$ –850.00	$ 25200.00
05/16/91		Sell	1	371.20			
05/23/91		SExit	1	377.50		$–3150.00	$ 22050.00
05/23/91		Buy	1	377.50			
05/28/91		LExit	1	379.15		$ 825.00	$ 22875.00
05/28/91		Sell	1	379.15			
05/30/91		SExit	1	383.90		$–2375.00	$ 20500.00
05/30/91		Buy	1	383.90			

NDX–SPX S&P 500 Index—CME–Daily 01/02/91–11/30/94

Date	Time	Type	Cnts	Price	Signal Name	Entry P/L	Cumulative
05/31/91		LExit	1	388.00		$ 2050.00	$ 22550.00
05/31/91		Sell	1	388.00			
06/04/91		SExit	1	387.75		$ 125.00	$ 22675.00
06/04/91		Buy	1	387.75			
06/06/91		LExit	1	386.30		$ −725.00	$ 21950.00
06/06/91		Sell	1	386.30			
06/10/91		SExit	1	380.50		$ 2900.00	$ 24850.00
06/10/91		Buy	1	380.50			
06/11/91		LExit	1	379.00		$ −750.00	$ 24100.00
06/11/91		Sell	1	379.00			
06/13/91		SExit	1	377.50		$ 750.00	$ 24850.00
06/13/91		Buy	1	377.50			
06/14/91		LExit	1	379.00		$ 750.00	$ 25600.00
06/14/91		Sell	1	379.00			
06/18/91		SExit	1	383.50		$−2250.00	$ 23350.00
06/18/91		Buy	1	383.50			
06/19/91		LExit	1	379.70		$−1900.00	$ 21450.00
06/19/91		Sell	1	379.70			
06/26/91		SExit	1	374.00		$ 2850.00	$ 24300.00
06/26/91		Buy	1	374.00			
07/02/91		LExit	1	380.10		$ 3050.00	$ 27350.00
07/02/91		Sell	1	380.10			
07/05/91		SExit	1	374.00		$ 3050.00	$ 30400.00
07/05/91		Buy	1	374.00			
07/08/91		LExit	1	374.30		$ 150.00	$ 30550.00
07/08/91		Sell	1	374.30			
07/09/91		SExit	1	380.20		$−2950.00	$ 27600.00
07/09/91		Buy	1	380.20			
07/12/91		LExit	1	381.50		$ 650.00	$ 28250.00
07/12/91		Sell	1	381.50			
07/15/91		SExit	1	383.00		$ −750.00	$ 27500.00
07/15/91		Buy	1	383.00			
07/16/91		LExit	1	384.50		$ 750.00	$ 28250.00
07/16/91		Sell	1	384.50			

NDX–SPX S&P 500 Index—CME–Daily 01/02/91–11/30/94

Date	Time	Type	Cnts	Price	Signal Name	Entry P/L	Cumulative
07/22/91		SExit	1	385.90		$ −700.00	$ 27550.00
07/22/91		Buy	1	385.90			
07/23/91		LExit	1	386.00		$ 50.00	$ 27600.00
07/23/91		Sell	1	386.00			
07/26/91		SExit	1	382.00		$ 2000.00	$ 29600.00
07/26/91		Buy	1	382.00			
07/30/91		LExit	1	385.10		$ 1550.00	$ 31150.00
07/30/91		Sell	1	385.10			
07/31/91		SExit	1	388.25		$−1575.00	$ 29575.00
07/31/91		Buy	1	388.25			
08/06/91		LExit	1	385.90		$−1175.00	$ 28400.00
08/06/91		Sell	1	385.90			
08/08/91		SExit	1	391.00		$−2550.00	$ 25850.00
08/08/91		Buy	1	391.00			
08/16/91		LExit	1	390.70		$ −150.00	$ 25700.00
08/16/91		Sell	1	390.70			
08/19/91		SExit	1	381.85		$ 4425.00	$ 30125.00
08/19/91		Buy	1	381.85			
08/21/91		LExit	1	385.50		$ 1825.00	$ 31950.00
08/21/91		Sell	1	385.50			
08/22/91		SExit	1	393.20		$−3850.00	$ 28100.00
08/22/91		Buy	1	393.20			
08/23/91		LExit	1	390.80		$−1200.00	$ 26900.00
08/23/91		Sell	1	390.80			
08/27/91		SExit	1	394.40		$−1800.00	$ 25100.00
08/27/91		Buy	1	394.40			
08/29/91		LExit	1	397.25		$ 1425.00	$ 26525.00
08/29/91		Sell	1	397.25			
09/04/91		SExit	1	393.10		$ 2075.00	$ 28600.00
09/04/91		Buy	1	393.10			
09/05/91		LExit	1	391.50		$ −800.00	$ 27800.00
09/05/91		Sell	1	391.50			
09/10/91		SExit	1	389.00		$ 1250.00	$ 29050.00
09/10/91		Buy	1	389.00			

NDX–SPX S&P 500 Index—CME–Daily 01/02/91–11/30/94

Date	Time	Type	Cnts	Price	Signal Name	Entry P/L	Cumulative
09/11/91		LExit	1	385.70		$–1650.00	$ 27400.00
09/11/91		Sell	1	385.70			
09/12/91		SExit	1	386.00		$ –150.00	$ 27250.00
09/12/91		Buy	1	386.00			
09/17/91		LExit	1	388.00		$ 1000.00	$ 28250.00
09/17/91		Sell	1	388.00			
09/19/91		SExit	1	389.00		$ –500.00	$ 27750.00
09/19/91		Buy	1	389.00			
09/27/91		LExit	1	389.70		$ 350.00	$ 28100.00
09/27/91		Sell	1	389.70			
10/07/91		SExit	1	382.50		$ 3600.00	$ 31700.00
10/07/91		Buy	1	382.50			
10/09/91		LExit	1	382.00		$ –250.00	$ 31450.00
10/09/91		Sell	1	382.00			
10/10/91		SExit	1	378.70		$ 1650.00	$ 33100.00
10/10/91		Buy	1	378.70			
10/11/91		LExit	1	382.30		$ 1800.00	$ 34900.00
10/11/91		Sell	1	382.30			
10/14/91		SExit	1	383.40		$ –550.00	$ 34350.00
10/14/91		Buy	1	383.40			
10/18/91		LExit	1	394.25		$ 5425.00	$ 39775.00
10/18/91		Sell	1	394.25			
10/21/91		SExit	1	393.50		$ 375.00	$ 40150.00
10/21/91		Buy	1	393.50			
10/24/91		LExit	1	389.10		$–2200.00	$ 37950.00
10/24/91		Sell	1	389.10			
10/30/91		SExit	1	393.10		$–2000.00	$ 35950.00
10/30/91		Buy	1	393.10			
11/01/91		LExit	1	393.00		$ –50.00	$ 35900.00
11/01/91		Sell	1	393.00			
11/06/91		SExit	1	389.10		$ 1950.00	$ 37850.00
11/06/91		Buy	1	389.10			
11/07/91		LExit	1	391.30		$ 1100.00	$ 38950.00
11/07/91		Sell	1	391.30			

NDX–SPX S&P 500 Index—CME–Daily 01/02/91–11/30/94

Date	Time	Type	Cnts	Price	Signal Name	Entry P/L	Cumulative
11/11/91		SExit	1	393.45		$–1075.00	$ 37875.00
11/11/91		Buy	1	393.45			
11/15/91		LExit	1	398.20		$ 2375.00	$ 40250.00
11/15/91		Sell	1	398.20			
11/19/91		SExit	1	382.90		$ 7650.00	$ 47900.00
11/19/91		Buy	1	382.90			
11/26/91		LExit	1	377.70		$–2600.00	$ 45300.00
11/26/91		Sell	1	377.70			
11/29/91		SExit	1	376.10		$ 800.00	$ 46100.00
11/29/91		Buy	1	376.10			
12/12/91		LExit	1	380.00		$ 1950.00	$ 48050.00
12/12/91		Sell	1	380.00			
12/16/91		SExit	1	386.20		$–3100.00	$ 44950.00
12/16/91		Buy	1	386.20			
12/18/91		LExit	1	384.65		$ –775.00	$ 44175.00
12/18/91		Sell	1	384.65			
12/26/91		SExit	1	401.10		$–8225.00	$ 35950.00
12/26/91		Buy	1	401.10			
01/06/92		LExit	1	419.50		$ 9200.00	$ 45150.00
01/06/92		Sell	1	419.50			
01/07/92		SExit	1	418.40		$ 550.00	$ 45700.00
01/07/92		Buy	1	418.40			
01/15/92		LExit	1	422.20		$ 1900.00	$ 47600.00
01/15/92		Sell	1	422.20			
01/16/92		SExit	1	421.00		$ 600.00	$ 48200.00
01/16/92		Buy	1	421.00			
01/17/92		LExit	1	419.50		$ –750.00	$ 47450.00
01/17/92		Sell	1	419.50			
01/23/92		SExit	1	419.60		$ –50.00	$ 47400.00
01/23/92		Buy	1	419.60			
01/27/92		LExit	1	417.10		$–1250.00	$ 46150.00
01/27/92		Sell	1	417.10			
01/29/92		SExit	1	414.60		$ 1250.00	$ 47400.00
01/29/92		Buy	1	414.60			

NDX–SPX S&P 500 Index—CME–Daily 01/02/91–11/30/94

Date	Time	Type	Cnts	Price	Signal Name	Entry P/L	Cumulative
02/03/92		LExit	I	408.25		$–3175.00	$ 44225.00
02/03/92		Sell	I	408.25			
02/04/92		SExit	I	410.10		$ –925.00	$ 43300.00
02/04/92		Buy	I	410.10.			
02/07/92		LExit	I	414.80		$ 2350.00	$ 45650.00
02/07/92		Sell	I	414.80			
02/10/92		SExit	I	412.70		$ 1050.00	$ 46700.00
02/10/92		Buy	I	412.70			
02/11/92		LExit	I	414.00		$ 650.00	$ 47350.00
02/11/92		Sell	I	414.00			
02/13/92		SExit	I	417.70		$–1850.00	$ 45500.00
02/13/92		Buy	I	417.70			
02/14/92		LExit	I	413.50		$–2100.00	$ 43400.00
02/14/92		Sell	I	413.50			
02/21/92		SExit	I	413.00		$ 250.00	$ 43650.00
02/21/92		Buy	I	413.00			
02/24/92		LExit	I	411.70		$ –650.00	$ 43000.00
02/24/92		Sell	I	411.70			
02/26/92		SExit	I	411.50		$ 100.00	$ 43100.00
02/26/92		Buy	I	411.50			
02/27/92		LExit	I	415.00		$ 1750.00	$ 44850.00
02/27/92		Sell	I	415.00			
02/28/92		SExit	I	415.80		$ –400.00	$ 44450.00
02/28/92		Buy	I	415.80			
03/02/92		LExit	I	412.30		$–1750.00	$ 42700.00
03/02/92		Sell	I	412.30			
03/03/92		SExit	I	412.75		$ –225.00	$ 42475.00
03/03/92		Buy	I	412.75			
03/04/92		LExit	I	412.70		$ –25.00	$ 42450.00
03/04/92		Sell	I	412.70			
03/11/92		SExit	I	406.50		$ 3100.00	$ 45550.00
03/11/92		Buy	I	406.50			
03/12/92		LExit	I	404.60		$ –950.00	$ 44600.00
03/12/92		Sell	I	404.60			

NDX–SPX S&P 500 Index—CME–Daily 01/02/91–11/30/94

Date	Time	Type	Cnts	Price	Signal Name	Entry P/L	Cumulative
03/17/92		SExit	1	408.40		$–1900.00	$ 42700.00
03/17/92		Buy	1	408.40			
03/20/92		LExit	1	410.80		$ 1200.00	$ 43900.00
03/20/92		Sell	1	410.80			
03/26/92		SExit	1	409.75		$ 525.00	$ 44425.00
03/26/92		Buy	1	409.75			
03/27/92		LExit	1	408.20		$ –775.00	$ 43650.00
03/27/92		Sell	1	408.20			
04/01/92		SExit	1	401.50		$ 3350.00	$ 47000.00
04/01/92		Buy	1	401.50			
04/03/92		LExit	1	400.20		$ –650.00	$ 46350.00
04/03/92		Sell	1	400.20			
04/07/92		SExit	1	406.00		$–2900.00	$ 43450.00
04/07/92		Buy	1	406.00			
04/08/92		LExit	1	396.25		$–4875.00	$ 38575.00
04/08/92		Sell	1	396.25			
04/09/92		SExit	1	395.85		$ 200.00	$ 38775.00
04/09/92		Buy	1	395.85			
04/13/92		LExit	1	404.75		$ 4450.00	$ 43225.00
04/13/92		Sell	1	404.75			
04/14/92		SExit	1	408.20		$–1725.00	$ 41500.00
04/14/92		Buy	1	408.20			
04/15/92		LExit	1	414.10		$ 2950.00	$ 44450.00
04/15/92		Sell	1	414.10			
04/16/92		SExit	1	417.30		$–1600.00	$ 42850.00
04/16/92		Buy	1	417.30			
04/20/92		LExit	1	413.50		$–1900.00	$ 40950.00
04/20/92		Seil	1	413.50			
04/23/92		SExit	1	410.10		$ 1700.00	$ 42650.00
04/23/92		Buy	1	410.10			
04/24/92		LExit	1	411.90		$ 900.00	$ 43550.00
04/24/92		Sell	1	411.90			
04/30/92		SExit	1	412.40		$ –250.00	$ 43300.00
04/30/92		Buy	1	412.40			

NDX–SPX S&P 500 Index—CME–Daily 01/02/91–11/30/94

Date	Time	Type	Cnts	Price	Signal Name	Entry P/L	Cumulative
05/05/92		LExit	1	416.30		$ 1950.00	$ 45250.00
05/05/92		Sell	1	416.30			
05/06/92		SExit	1	417.90		$ −800.00	$ 44450.00
05/06/92		Buy	1	417.90			
05/08/92		LExit	1	416.60		$ −650.00	$ 43800.00
05/08/92		Sell	1	416.60			
05/13/92		SExit	1	416.40		$ 100.00	$ 43900.00
05/13/92		Buy	1	416.40			
05/14/92		LExit	1	415.30		$ −550.00	$ 43350.00
05/14/92		Sell	1	415.30			
05/18/92		SExit	1	412.10		$ 1600.00	$ 44950.00
05/18/92		Buy	1	412.10			
05/19/92		LExit	1	413.70		$ 800.00	$ 45750.00
05/19/92		Sell	1	413.70			
05/21/92		SExit	1	414.30		$ −300.00	$ 45450.00
05/21/92		Buy	1	414.30			
05/26/92		LExit	1	412.70		$ −800.00	$ 44650.00
05/26/92		Sell	1	412.70			
05/27/92		SExit	1	411.45		$ 625.00	$ 45275.00
05/27/92		Buy	1	411.45			
05/29/92		LExit	1	417.30		$ 2925.00	$ 48200.00
05/29/92		Sell	1	417.30			
06/01/92		SExit	1	414.40		$ 1450.00	$ 49650.00
06/01/92		Buy	1	414.40			
06/04/92		LExit	1	414.65		$ 125.00	$ 49775.00
06/04/92		Sell	1	414.65			
06/11/92		SExit	1	407.80		$ 3425.00	$ 53200.00
06/11/92		Buy	1	407.80			
06/12/92		LExit	1	413.00		$ 2600.00	$ 55800.00
06/12/92		Sell	1	413.00			
06/15/92		SExit	1	409.00		$ 2000.00	$ 57800.00
06/15/92		Buy	1	409.00			
06/16/92		LExit	1	411.50		$ 1250.00	$ 59050.00
06/16/92		Sell	1	411.50			

NDX–SPX S&P 500 Index—CME–Daily 01/02/91–11/30/94

Date	Time	Type	Cnts	Price	Signal Name	Entry P/L	Cumulative
06/18/92		SExit	1	402.10		$ 4700.00	$ 63750.00
06/18/92		Buy	1	402.10			
06/19/92		LExit	1	403.20		$ 550.00	$ 64300.00
06/19/92		Sell	1	403.20			
06/22/92		SExit	1	402.00		$ 600.00	$ 64900.00
06/22/92		Buy	1	402.00			
06/23/92		LExit	1	404.25		$ 1125.00	$ 66025.00
06/23/92		Sell	1	404.25;			
06/24/92		SExit	1	404.30		$ −25.00	$ 66000.00
06/24/92		Buy	1	404.30			
06/25/92		LExit	1	406.20		$ 950.00	$ 66950.00
06/25/92		Sell	1	406.20			
06/30/92		SExit	1	409.20		$−1500.00	$ 65450.00
06/30/92		Buy	1	409.20			
07/06/92		LExit	1	412.30		$ 1550.00	$ 67000.00
07/06/92		Sell	1	412.30			
07/09/92		SExit	1	410.75		$ 775.00	$ 67775.00
07/09/92		Buy	1	410.75			
07/20/92		LExit	1	411.50		$ 375.00	$ 68150.00
07/20/92		Sell	1	411.50			
07/22/92		SExit	1	411.40		$ 50.00	$ 68200.00
07/22/92		Buy	1	411.40			
07/23/92		LExit	1	410.50		$ −450.00	$ 67750.00
07/23/92		Sell	1	410.50			
07/24/92		SExit	1	410.70		$ −100.00	$ 67650.00
07/24/92		Buy	1	410.70			
07/28/92		LExit	1	411.90		$ 600.00	$ 68250.00
07/28/92		Sell	1	411.90			
08/04/92		SExit	1	424.70		$−6400.00	$ 61850.00
08/04/92		Buy	1	424.70			
08/05/92		LExit	1	422.95		$ −875.00	$ 60975.00
08/05/92		Sell	1	422.95			
08/10/92		SExit	1	416.80		$ 3075.00	$ 64050.00
08/10/92		Buy	1	416.80			

NDX–SPX S&P 500 Index—CME–Daily 01/02/91–11/30/94

Date	Time	Type	Cnts	Price	Signal Name	Entry P/L	Cumulative
08/12/92		LExit	1	418.55		$ 875.00	$ 64925.00
08/12/92		Sell	1	418.55			
08/14/92		SExit	1	418.40		$ 75.00	$ 65000.00
08/14/92		Buy	1	418.40			
08/17/92		LExit	1	420.35		$ 975.00	$ 65975.00
08/17/92		Sell	1	420.35			
08/20/92		SExit	1	418.70		$ 825.00	$ 66800.00
08/20/92		Buy	1	418.70			
08/24/92		LExit	1	412.00		$–3350.00	$ 63450.00
08/24/92		Sell	1	412.00			
08/26/92		SExit	1	411.70		$ 150.00	$ 63600.00
08/26/92		Buy	1	411.70			
08/31/92		LExit	1	414.80		$ 1550.00	$ 65150.00
08/31/92		Sell	1	414.80			
09/01/92		SExit	1	413.75		$ 525.00	$ 65675.00
09/01/92		Buy	1	413.75			
09/08/92		LExit	1	416.25		$ 1250.00	$ 66925.00
09/08/92		Sell	1	416.25			
09/09/92		SExit	1	414.50		$ 875.00	$ 67800.00
09/09/92		Buy	1	414.50			
09/17/92		LExit	1	421.00		$ 3250.00	$ 71050.00
09/17/92		Sell	1	421.00			
09/18/92		SExit	1	420.60		$ 200.00	$ 71250.00
09/18/92		Buy	1	420.60			
09/21/92		LExit	1	423.00		$ 1200.00	$ 72450.00
09/21/92		Sell	1	423.00			
09/22/92		SExit	1	421.80		$ 600.00	$ 73050.00
09/22/92		Buy	1	421.80			
09/28/92		LExit	1	413.60		$–4100.00	$ 68950.00
09/28/92		Sell	1	413.60			
09/30/92		SExit	1	416.80		$–1600.00	$ 67350.00
09/30/92		Buy	1	416.80			
10/02/92		LExit	1	416.00		$ –400.00	$ 66950.00
10/02/92		Sell	1	416.00			

NDX–SPX S&P 500 Index—CME–Daily 01/02/91–11/30/94

Date	Time	Type	Cnts	Price	Signal Name	Entry P/L	Cumulative
10/05/92		SExit	1	408.20		$ 3900.00	$ 70850.00
10/05/92		Buy	1	408.20			
10/09/92		LExit	1	406.00		$–1100.00	$ 69750.00
10/09/92		Sell	1	406.00			
10/12/92		SExit	1	404.55		$ 725.00	$ 70475.00
10/12/92		Buy	1	404.55			
10/13/92		LExit	1	407.70		$ 1575.00	$ 72050.00
10/13/92		Sell	1	407.70			
10/14/92		SExit	1	408.30		$ –300.00	$ 71750.00
10/14/92		Buy	1	408.30			
10/15/92		LExit	1	407.10		$ –600.00	$ 71150.00
10/15/92		Sell	1	407.10			
10/16/92		SExit	1	410.85		$–1875.00	$ 69275.00
10/16/92		Buy	1	410.85			
10/27/92		LExit	1	418.80		$ 3975.00	$ 73250.00
10/27/92		Sell	1	418.80			
10/29/92		SExit	1	420.40		$ –800.00	$ 72450.00
10/29/92		Buy	1	420.40			
11/03/92		LExit	1	421.90		$ 750.00	$ 73200.00
11/03/92		Sell	1	421.90			
11/05/92		SExit	1	416.50		$ 2700.00	$ 75900.00
11/05/92		Buy	1	416.50			
11/12/92		LExit	1	422.40		$ 2950.00	$ 78850.00
11/12/92		Sell	1	422.40			
11/16/92		SExit	1	422.75		$ –175.00	$ 78675.00
11/16/92		Buy	1	422.75			
11/17/92		LExit	1	421.20		$ –775.00	$ 77900.00
11/17/92		Sell	1	421.20			
11/19/92		SExit	1	422.50		$ –650.00	$ 77250.00
11/19/92		Buy	1	422.50			
11/23/92		LExit	1	426.15		$ 1825.00	$ 79075.00
11/23/92		Sell	1	426.15			
11/25/92		SExit	1	428.00		$ –925.00	$ 78150.00
11/25/92		Buy	1	428.00			

NDX–SPX S&P 500 Index—CME–Daily 01/02/91–11/30/94

Date	Time	Type	Cnts	Price	Signal Name	Entry P/L	Cumulative
11/27/92		LExit	1	429.70		$ 850.00	$ 79000.00
11/27/92		Sell	1	429.70			
12/01/92		SExit	1	430.80		$ −550.00	$ 78450.00
12/01/92		Buy	1	430.80			
12/03/92		LExit	1	430.20		$ −300.00	$ 78150.00
12/03/92		Sell	1	430.20			
12/04/92		SExit	1	431.30		$ −550.00	$ 77600.00
12/04/92		Buy	1	431.30			
12/09/92		LExit	1	436.95		$ 2825.00	$ 80425.00
12/09/92		Sell	1	436.95			
12/17/92		SExit	1	432.60		$ 2175.00	$ 82600.00
12/17/92		Buy	1	432.60			
12/21/92		LExit	1	440.95		$ 4175.00	$ 86775.00
12/21/92		Sell	1	440.95			
12/22/92		SExit	1	442.30		$ −675.00	$ 86100.00
12/22/92		Buy	1	442.30			
12/23/92		LExit	1	441.35		$ −475.00	$ 85625.00
12/23/92		Sell	1	441.35			
12/24/92		SExit	1	440.60		$ 375.00	$ 86000.00
12/24/92		Buy	1	440.60			
12/31/92		LExit	1	439.20		$ −700.00	$ 85300.00
12/31/92		Sell	1	439.20			
01/04/93		SExit	1	438.25		$ 475.00	$ 85775.00
01/04/93		Buy	1	438.25			
01/05/93		LExit	1	435.60		$ −1325.00	$ 84450.00
01/05/93		Sell	1	435.60			
01/06/93		SExit	1	434.60		$ 500.00	$ 84950.00
01/06/93		Buy	1	434.60			
01/13/93		LExit	1	431.40		$ −1600.00	$ 83350.00
01/13/93		Sell	1	431.40			
01/14/93		SExit	1	434.20		$ −1400.00	$ 81950.00
01/14/93		Buy	1	434.20			
01/18/93		LExit	1	436.60		$ 1200.00	$ 83150.00
01/18/93		Sell	1	436.60			

NDX–SPX S&P 500 Index—CME–Daily 01/02/91–11/30/94

Date	Time	Type	Cnts	Price	Signal Name	Entry P/L	Cumulative
01/21/93		SExit	1	433.30		$ 1650.00	$ 84800.00
01/21/93		Buy	1	433.30			
01/25/93		LExit	1	436.30		$ 1500.00	$ 86300.00
01/25/93		Sell	1	436.30			
02/02/93		SExit	1	441.70		$–2700.00	$ 83600.00
02/02/93		Buy	1	441.70			
02/04/93		LExit	1	449.10		$ 3700.00	$ 87300.00
02/04/93		Sell	1	449.10			
02/11/93		SExit	1	447.30		$ 900.00	$ 88200.00
02/11/93		Byy	1	447.30			
02/12/93		LExit	1	447.75		$ 225.00	$ 88425.00
02/12/93		Sell	1	447.75			
02/19/93		SExit	1	433.50		$ 7125.00	$ 95550.00
02/19/93		Buy	1	433.50			
02/22/93		LExit	1	435.40		$ 950.00	$ 96500.00
02/22/93		Sell	1	435.40			
02/24/93		SExit	1	436.00		$ –300.00	$ 96200.00
02/24/93		Buy	1	436.00			
03/01/93		LExit	1	444.30		$ 4150.00	$100350.00
03/01/93		Sell	1	444.30			
03/03/93		SExit	1	448.60		$–2150.00	$ 98200.00
03/03/93		Buy	1	448.60			
03/05/93		LExit	1	448.00		$ –300.00	$ 97900.00
03/05/93		Sell	1	448.00			
03/08/93		SExit	1	447.30		$ 350.00	$ 98250.00
03/08/93		Buy	1	447.30			
03/09/93		LExit	1	455.50		$ 4100.00	$102350.00
03/09/93		Sell	1	455.50			
03/10/93		SExit	1	455.00		$ 250.00	$102600.00
03/10/93		Buy	1	455.00			
03/11/93		LExit	1	456.05		$ 525.00	$103125.00
03/11/93		Sell	1	456.05			
03/12/93		SExit	1	452.00		$ 2025.00	$105150.00
03/12/93		Buy	1	452.00			

NDX–SPX S&P 500 Index—CME–Daily 01/02/91–11/30/94

Date	Time	Type	Cnts	Price	Signal Name	Entry P/L	Cumulative
03/17/93		LExit	1	450.60		$ −700.00	$104450.00
03/17/93		Sell	1	450.60			
03/25/93		SExit	1	448.90		$ 850.00	$105300.00
03/25/93		Buy	1	448.90			
03/30/93		LExit	1	451.70		$ 1400.00	$106700.00
03/30/93		Sell	1	451.70			
03/31/93		SExit	1	453.40		$ −850.00	$105850.00
03/31/93		Buy	1	453.40			
04/02/93		LExit	1	447.00		$−3200.00	$102650.00
04/02/93		Sell	1	447.00			
04/06/93		SExit	1	443.50		$ 1750.00	$104400.00
04/06/93		Buy	1	443.50			
04/07/93		LExit	1	442.50		$ −500.00	$103900.00
04/07/93		Sell	1	442.50			
04/08/93		SExit	1	445.00		$−1250.00	$102650.00
04/08/93		Buy	1	445.00			
04/12/93		LExit	1	446.00		$ 500.00	$103150.00
04/12/93		Sell	1	446.00			
04/13/93		SExit	1	448.00		$−1000.00	$102150.00
04/13/93		Buy	1	448.00			
04/14/93		LExit	1	449.65		$ 825.00	$102975.00
04/14/93		Sell	1	449.65			
04/15/93		SExit	1	448.70		$ 475.00	$103450.00
04/15/93		Buy	1	448.70			
04/16/93		LExit	1	449.00		$ 150.00	$103600.00
04/16/93		Sell	1	449.00			
04/21/93		SExit	1	445.50		$ 1750.00	$105350.00
04/21/93		Buy	1	445.50			
04/26/93		LExit	1	436.50		$−4500.00	$100850.00
04/26/93		Sell	1	436.50			
04/28/93		SExit	1	436.90		$ −200.00	$100650.00
04/28/93		Buy	1	436.90			
04/30/93		LExit	1	440.00		$ 1550.00	$102200.00
04/30/93		Sell	1	440.00			

NDX–SPX S&P 500 Index—CME–Daily 01/02/91–11/30/94

Date	Time	Type	Cnts	Price	Signal Name	Entry P/L	Cumulative
05/04/93		SExit	1	442.60		$–1300.00	$100900.00
05/04/93		Buy	1	442.60			
05/07/93		LExit	1	443.70		$ 550.00	$101450.00
05/07/93		Sell	1	443.70			
05/10/93		SExit	1	442.70		$ 500.00	$101950.00
05/10/93		Buy	1	442.70			
05/12/93		LExit	1	443.00		$ 150.00	$102100.00
05/12/93		Sell	1	443.00			
05/14/93		SExit	1	438.90		$ 2050.00	$104150.00
05/14/93		Buy	1	438.90			
05/25/93		LExit	1	448.85		$ 4975.00	$109125.00
05/25/93		Sell	1	448.85			
05/27/93		SExit	1	454.20		$–2675.00	$106450.00
05/27/93		Buy	1	454.20			
05/28/93		LExit	1	451.60		$–1300.00	$105150.00
05/28/93		Sell	1	451.60			
06/02/93		SExit	1	453.20		$ –800.00	$104350.00
06/02/93		Buy	1	453.20			
06/07/93		LExit	1	451.50		$ –850.00	$103500.00
06/07/93		Sell	1	451.50			
06/14/93		SExit	1	448.50		$ 1500.00	$105000.00
06/14/93		Buy	1	448.50			
06/17/93		LExit	1	448.90		$ 200.00	$105200.00
06/17/93		Sell	1	448.90			
06/24/93		SExit	1	443.80		$ 2550.00	$107750.00
06/24/93		Buy	1	443.80			
06/25/93		LExit	1	448.30		$ 2250.00	$110000.00
06/25/93		Sell	1	448.30			
06/28/93		SExit	1	450.20		$ –950.00	$109050.00
06/28/93		Buy	1	450.20			
06/30/93		LExit	1	451.50		$ 650.00	$109700.00
06/30/93		Sell	1	451.50			
07/01/93		SExit	1	451.30		$ 100.00	$109800.00
07/01/93		Buy	1	451.30			

NDX–SPX S&P 500 Index—CME—Daily 01/02/91–11/30/94

Date	Time	Type	Cnts	Price	Signal Name	Entry P/L	Cumulative
07/02/93		LExit	1	448.50		$–1400.00	$108400.00
07/02/93		Sell	1	448.50			
07/06/93		SExit	1	447.05		$ 725.00	$109125.00
07/06/93		Buy	1	447.05			
07/08/93		LExit	1	443.90		$–1575.00	$107550.00
07/08/93		Sell	1	443.90			
07/12/93		SExit	1	449.10		$–2600.00	$104950.00
07/12/93		Buy	1	449.10			
07/13/93		LExit	1	449.60		$ 250.00	$105200.00
07/13/93		Sell	1	449.60			
07/14/93		SExit	1	449.10		$ 250.00	$105450.00
07/14/93		Buy	1	449.10			
07/15/93		LExit	1	449.40		$ 150.00	$105600.00
07/15/93		Sell	1	449.40			
07/21/93		SExit	1	446.90		$ 1250.00	$106850.00
07/21/93		Buy	1	446.90			
07/22/93		LExit	1	446.70		$ –100.00	$106750.00
07/22/93		Sell	1	446.70			
07/26/93		SExit	1	447.70		$ –500.00	$106250.00
07/26/93		Buy	1	447.70			
07/28/93		LExit	1	447.80		$ 50.00	$106300.00
07/28/93		Sell	1	447.80			
07/29/93		SExit	1	448.80		$ –500.00	$105800.00
07/29/93		Buy	1	448.80			
07/30/93		LExit	1	450.10		$ 650.00	$106450.00
07/30/93		Sell	1	450.10			
08/03/93		SExit	1	449.80		$ 150.00	$106600.00
08/03/93		Buy	1	449.80			
08/10/93		LExit	1	450.40		$ 300.00	$106900.00
08/10/93		Sell	1	450.40			
08/12/93		SExit	1	451.60		$ –600.00	$106300.00
08/12/93		Buy	1	451.60			
08/16/93		LExit	1	450.20		$ –700.00	$105600.00
08/16/93		Sell	1	450.20			

NDX–SPX S&P 500 Index—CME–Daily 01/02/91–11/30/94

Date	Time	Type	Cnts	Price	Signal Name	Entry P/L	Cumulative
08/17/93		SExit	1	451.75		$ −775.00	$104825.00
08/17/93		Buy	1	451.75			
08/19/93		LExit	1	456.30		$ 2275.00	$107100.00
08/19/93		Sell	1	456.30			
08/23/93		SExit	1	454.70		$ 800.00	$107900.00
08/23/93		Buy	1	454.70			
08/25/93		LExit	1	460.40		$ 2850.00	$110750.00
08/25/93		Sell	1	460.40			
08/30/93		SExit	1	460.90		$ −250.00	$110500.00
08/30/93		Buy	1	460.90			
09/07/93		LExit	1	461.10		$ 100.00	$110600.00
09/07/93		Sell	1	461.10			
09/09/93		SExit	1	455.00		$ 3050.00	$113650.00
09/09/93		Buy	1	455.00			
09/13/93		LExit	1	463.50		$ 4250.00	$117900.00
09/13/93		Sell	1	463.50			
09/16/93		SExit	1	460.60		$ 1450.00	$119350.00
09/16/93		Buy	1	460.60			
10/01/93		LExit	1	459.35		$ −625.00	$118725.00
10/01/93		Sell	1	459.35			
10/05/93		SExit	1	462.25		$−1450.00	$117275.00
10/05/93		Buy	1	462.25			
10/06/93		LExit	1	461.40		$ −425.00	$116850.00
10/06/93		Sell	1	461.40			
10/11/93		SExit	1	461.40		$ 0.00	$116850.00
10/11/93		Buy	1	461.40			
10/12/93		LExit	1	461.95		$ 275.00	$117125.00
10/12/93		Sell	1	461.95			
10/13/93		SExit	1	461.85		$ 50.00	$117175.00
10/13/93		Buy	1	461.85			
10/18/93		LExit	1	470.15		$ 4150.00	$121325.00
10/18/93		Sell	1	470.15			
10/21/93		SExit	1	467.20		$ 1475.00	$122800.00
10/21/93		Buy	1	467.20			

NDX–SPX S&P 500 Index—CME–Daily 01/02/91–11/30/94

Date	Time	Type	Cnts	Price	Signal Name	Entry P/L	Cumulative
10/26/93		LExit	1	464.50		$–1350.00	$121450.00
10/26/93		Sell	1	464.50			
10/28/93		SExit	1	465.80		$ –650.00	$120800.00
10/28/93		Buy	1	465.80			
10/29/93		LExit	1	467.95		$ 1075.00	$121875.00
10/29/93		Sell	1	467.95			
11/01/93		SExit	1	467.40		$ 275.00	$122150.00
11/01/93		Buy	1	467.40			
11/04/93		LExit	1	462.80		$–2300.00	$119850.00
11/04/93		Sell	1	462.80			
11/08/93		SExit	1	459.80		$ 1500.00	$121350.00
11/08/93		Buy	1	459.80			
11/15/93		LExit	1	466.10		$ 3150.00	$124500.00
11/15/93		Sell	1	466.10			
11/24/93		SExit	1	462.40		$ 1850.00	$126350.00
11/24/93		Buy	1	462.40			
11/30/93		LExit	1	461.40		$ –500.00	$125850.00
11/30/93		Sell	1	461.40			
12/01/93		SExit	1	463.80		$–1200.00	$124650.00
12/01/93		Buy	1	463.80			
12/07/93		LExit	1	466.60		$ 1400.00	$126050.00
12/07/93		Sell	1	466.60			
12/16/93		SExit	1	463.70		$ 1450.00	$127500.00
12/16/93		Buy	1	463.70			
12/17/93		LExit	1	465.45		$ 875.00	$128375.00
12/17/93		Sell	1	465.45			
12/21/93		SExit	1	467.00		$ –775.00	$127600.00
12/21/93		Buy	1	467.00			
12/22/93		LExit	1	467.20		$ 100.00	$127700.00
12/22/93		Sell	1	467.20			
12/27/93		SExit	1	468.90		$ –850.00	$126850.00
12/27/93		Buy	1	468.90			
12/28/93		LExit	1	471.10		$ 1100.00	$127950.00
12/28/93		Sell	1	471.10			

NDX–SPX S&P 500 Index—CME–Daily 01/02/91–11/30/94

Date	Time	Type	Cnts	Price	Signal Name	Entry P/L	Cumulative
12/29/93		SExit	1	472.10		$ –500.00	$127450.00
12/29/93		Buy	1	472.10			
01/04/94		LExit	1	465.80		$–3150.00	$124300.00
01/04/94		Sell	1	465.80			
01/05/94		SExit	1	467.00		$ –600.00	$123700.00
01/05/94		Buy	1	467.00			
01/10/94		LExit	1	470.80		$ 1900.00	$125600.00
01/10/94		Sell	1	470.80			
01/12/94		SExit	1	475.35		$–2275.00	$123325.00
01/12/94		Buy	1	475.35			
01/19/94		LExit	1	473.90		$ –725.00	$122600.00
01/19/94		Sell	1	473.90			
01/21/94		SExit	1	475.10		$ –600.00	$122000.00
01/21/94		Buy	1	475.10			
01/26/94		LExit	1	471.50		$–1800.00	$120200.00
01/26/94		Sell	1	471.50			
01/31/94		SExit	1	480.20		$–4350.00	$115850.00
01/31/94		Buy	1	480.20			
02/01/94		LExit	1	481.30		$ 550.00	$116400.00
02/01/94		Sell	1	481.30			
02/08/94		SExit	1	472.10		$ 4600.00	$121000.00
02/08/94		Buy	1	472.10			
02/14/94		LExit	1	470.00		$–1050.00	$119950.00
02/14/94		Sell	1	470.00			
02/15/94		SExit	1	471.50		$ –750.00	$119200.00
02/15/94		Buy	1	471.50			
02/23/94		LExit	1	472.40		$ 450.00	$119650.00
02/23/94		Sell	1	472.40			
02/25/94		SExit	1	465.20		$ 3600.00	$123250.00
02/25/94		Buy	1	465.20			
03/03/94		LExit	1	464.50		$ –350.00	$122900.00
03/03/94		Sell	1	464.50			
03/04/94		SExit	1	463.80		$ 350.00	$123250.00
03/04/94		Buy	1	463.80			

NDX–SPX S&P 500 Index—CME–Daily 01/02/91–11/30/94

Date	Time	Type	Cnts	Price	Signal Name	Entry P/L	Cumulative
03/09/94		LExit	1	465.60		$ 900.00	$124150.00
03/09/94		Sell	1	465.60			
03/15/94		SExit	1	467.60		$–1000.00	$123150.00
03/15/94		Buy	1	467.60			
03/21/94		LExit	1	469.60		$ 1000.00	$124150.00
03/21/94		Sell	1	469.60			
03/24/94		SExit	1	469.00		$ 300.00	$124450.00
03/24/94		Buy	1	469.00			
03/25/94		LExit	1	465.50		$–1750.00	$122700.00
03/25/94		Sell	1	465.50			
03/31/94		SExit	1	446.00		$ 9750.00	$132450.00
03/31/94		Buy	1	446.00			
04/05/94		LExit	1	443.00		$–1500.00	$130950.00
04/05/94		Sell	1	443.00			
04/06/94		SExit	1	449.25		$–3125.00	$127825.00
04/06/94		Buy	1	449.25			
04/07/94		LExit	1	448.00		$ –625.00	$127200.00
04/07/94		Sell	1	448.00			
04/18/94		SExit	1	445.75		$ 1125.00	$128325.00
04/18/94		Buy	1	445.75			
04/19/94		LExit	1	442.40		$–1675.00	$126650.00
04/19/94		Sell	1	442.40			
04/22/94		SExit	1	449.00		$–3300.00	$123350.00
04/22/94		Buy	1	449.00			
04/29/94		LExit	1	447.60		$ –700.00	$122650.00
04/29/94		Sell	1	447.60			
05/03/94		SExit	1	452.80		$–2600.00	$120050.00
05/03/94		Buy	1	452.80			
05/04/94		LExit	1	452.50		$ –150.00	$119900.00
05/04/94		Sell	1	452.50			
05/05/94		SExit	1	451.30		$ 600.00	$120500.00
05/05/94		Buy	1	451.30			
05/09/94		LExit	1	445.10		$–3100.00	$117400.00
05/09/94		Sell	1	445.10			

NDX–SPX S&P 500 Index—CME–Daily 01/02/91–11/30/94

Date	Time	Type	Cnts	Price	Signal Name	Entry P/L	Cumulative
05/19/94		SExit	1	453.40		$–4150.00	$113250.00
05/19/94		Buy	1	453.40			
05/26/94		LExit	1	455.30		$ 950.00	$114200.00
05/26/94		Sell	1	455.30			
05/31/94		SExit	1	455.20		$ 50.00	$114250.00
05/31/94		Buy	1	455.20			
06/02/94		LExit	1	457.80		$ 1300.00	$115550.00
06/02/94		Sell	1	457.80			
06/03/94		SExit	1	457.20		$ 300.00	$115850.00
06/03/94		Buy	1	457.20			
06/06/94		LExit	1	460.90		$ 1850.00	$117700.00
06/06/94		Sell	1	460.90			
06/07/94		SExit	1	458.60		$ 1150.00	$118850.00
06/07/94		Buy	1	458.60			
06/08/94		LExit	1	459.50		$ 450.00	$119300.00
06/08/94		Sell	1	459.50			
06/13/94		SExit	1	458.20		$ 650.00	$119950.00
06/13/94		Buy	1	458.20			
06/14/94		LExit	1	460.00		$ 900.00	$120850.00
06/14/94		Sell	1	460.00			
06/15/94		SExit	1	462.70		$–1350.00	$119500.00
06/15/94		Buy	1	462.70			
06/17/94		LExit	1	463.05		$ 175.00	$119675.00
06/17/94		Sell	1	463.05			
06/23/94		SExit	1	454.30		$ 4375.00	$124050.00
06/23/94		Buy	1	454.30			
06/24/94		LExit	1	450.50		$–1900.00	$122150.00
06/24/94		Sell	1	450.50			
06/27/94		SExit	1	442.30		$ 4100.00	$126250.00
06/27/94		Buy	1	442.30			
06/30/94		LExit	1	449.40		$ 3550.00	$129800.00
06/30/94		Sell	1	449.40			
07/01/94		SExit	1	446.80		$ 1300.00	$131100.00
07/01/94		Buy	1	446.80			

NDX–SPX S&P 500 Index—CME–Daily 01/02/91–11/30/94

Date	Time	Type	Cnts	Price	Signal Name	Entry P/L	Cumulative
07/05/94		LExit	1	446.50		$ −150.00	$130950.00
07/05/94		Sell	1	446.50			
07/08/94		SExit	1	449.80		$−1650.00	$129300.00
07/08/94		Buy	1	449.80.			
07/11/94		LExit	1	449.90		$ 50.00	$129350.00
07/11/94		Sell	1	449.90			
07/12/94		SExit	1	448.60		$ 650.00	$130000.00
07/12/94		Buy	1	448.60			
07/15/94		LExit	1	453.90		$ 2650.00	$132650.00
07/15/94		Sell	1	453.90			
07/22/94		SExit	1	453.80		$ 50.00	$132700.00
07/22/94		Buy	1	453.80			
07/26/94		LExit	1	453.90		$ 50.00	$132750.00
07/26/94		Sell	1	453.90			
08/01/94		SExit	1	458.60		$−2350.00	$130400.00
08/01/94		Buy	1	458.60			
08/03/94		LExit	1	460.80		$ 1100.00	$131500.00
08/03/94		Sell	1	460.80			
08/05/94		SExit	1	456.60		$ 2100.00	$133600.00
08/05/94		Buy	1	456.60			
08/15/94		LExit	1	462.20		$ 2800.00	$136400.00
08/15/94		Sell	1	462.20			
08/16/94		SExit	1	461.90		$ 150.00	$136550.00
08/16/94		Buy	1	461.90			
08/17/94		LExit	1	465.70		$ 1900.00	$138450.00
08/17/94		Sell	1	465.70			
08/18/94		SExit	1	463.80		$ 950.00	$139400.00
08/18/94		Buy	1	463.80			
08/22/94		LExit	1	462.80		$ −500.00	$138900.00
08/22/94		Sell	1	462.80			
08/23/94		SExit	1	463.55		$ −375.00	$138525.00
08/23/94		Buy	1	463.55			
08/25/94		LExit	1	469.10		$ 2775.00	$141300.00
08/25/94		Sell	1	469.10			

NDX–SPX S&P 500 Index—CME–Daily 01/02/91–11/30/94

Date	Time	Type	Cnts	Price	Signal Name	Entry P/L	Cumulative
08/26/94		SExit	1	470.00		$ −450.00	$140850.00
08/26/94		Buy	1	470.00			
08/30/94		LExit	1	474.85		$ 2425.00	$143275.00
08/30/94		Sell	1	474.85			
08/31/94		SExit	1	475.50		$ −325.00	$142950.00
08/31/94		Buy	1	475.50			
09/01/94		LExit	1	473.80		$ −850.00	$142100.00
09/01/94		Sell	1	473.80			
09/06/94		SExit	1	471.00		$ 1400.00	$143500.00
09/06/94		Buy	1	471.00			
09/12/94		LExit	1	470.30		$ −350.00	$143150.00
09/12/94		Sell	1	470.30			
09/14/94		SExit	1	468.80		$ 750.00	$143900.00
09/14/94		Buy	1	468.80			
09/15/94		LExit	1	470.70		$ 950.00	$144850.00
09/15/94		Sell	1	470.70			
09/16/94		SExit	1	472.25		$ −775.00	$144075.00
09/16/94		Buy	1	472.25			
09/20/94		LExit	1	470.00		$−1125.00	$142950.00
09/20/94		Sell	1	470.00			
09/21/94		SExit	1	464.80		$ 2600.00	$145550.00
09/21/94		Buy	1	464.80			
09/22/94		LExit	1	463.60		$ −600.00	$144950.00
09/22/94		Sell	1	463.60			
09/23/94		SExit	1	463.25		$ 175.00	$145125.00
09/23/94		Buy	1	463.25			
09/26/94		LExit	1	462.20		$ −525.00	$144600.00
09/26/94		Sell	1	462.20			
09/30/94		SExit	1	464.20		$−1000.00	$143600.00
09/30/94		Buy	1	464.20			
10/04/94		LExit	1	464.30		$ 50.00	$143650.00
10/04/94		Sell	1	464.30			
10/06/94		SExit	1	455.20		$ 4550.00	$148200.00
10/06/94		Buy	1	455.20			

NDX–SPX S&P 500 Index—CME–Daily 01/02/91–11/30/94

Date	Time	Type	Cnts	Price	Signal Name	Entry P/L	Cumulative
10/07/94		LExit	1	453.40		$ −900.00	$147300.00
10/07/94		Sell	1	453.40			
10/10/94		SExit	1	457.00		$−1800.00	$145500.00
10/10/94		Buy	1	457.00			
10/13/94		LExit	1	467.50		$ 5250.00	$150750.00
10/13/94		Sell	1	467.50			
10/19/94		SExit	1	468.45		$ −475.00	$150275.00
10/19/94		Buy	1	468.45			
10/24/94		LExit	1	465.85		$−1300.00	$148975.00
10/24/94		Sell	1	465.85			
10/25/94		SExit	1	462.05		$ 1900.00	$150875.00
10/25/94		Buy	1	462.05			
10/26/94		LExit	1	462.30		$ 125.00	$151000.00
10/26/94		Sell	1	462.30			
10/27/94		SExit	1	463.35		$ −525.00	$150475.00
10/27/934		Buy	1	463.35			
10/28/94		LExit	1	467.20		$ 1925.00	$152400.00
10/28/94		Sell	1	467.20			
11/01/94		SExit	1	472.65		$−2725.00	$149675.00
11/01/94		Buy	1	472.65			
11/04/94		LExit	1	468.80		$−1925.00	$147750.00
11/04/94		Sell	1	468.80			
11/09/94		SExit	1	469.95		$ −575.00	$147175.00
11/09/94		Buy	1	469.95			
11/11/94		LExit	1	465.25		$−2350.00	$144825.00
11/11/94		Sell	1	465.25			
11/14/94		SExit	1	462.85		$ 1200.00	$146025.00
11/14/94		Buy	1	462.85			
11/23/94		LExit	1	446.60		$−8125.00	$137900.00
11/23/94		Sell	1	446.60			
11/28/94		SExit	1	454.95		$−4175.00	$133725.00
11/28/94		Buy	1	454.95			

Reprinted with permission of Omega Research Inc.

Chapter Seven

- •
- •
- •
- •
- •

Why Most Traders Lose

When a man knows he is to be hanged in a fortnight,
it concentrates his mind wonderfully.

Dr. Johnson

This is by far the most important chapter in this book. Unless the trader/investor learns how to take a loss, he or she will never be successful at this game. Too many traders will make money trade after trade, only to watch their profits evaporate when one trade moves against them. These traders all eventually blow up.

We are obsessed with money management. We are vigilantes when it comes to losses. We view losses the same way we view cancer. A small cancer can be removed, and the patient will most likely live. A small cancer allowed to grow into a large cancer will eventually kill the patient. A small loss removed early will most likely allow the trader to trade again. A small loss allowed to grow into a large loss will kill the trader. This may sound harsh. Unfortunately, it is reality. How many large losses can one take before his or her trading days are over?

FOUR DISEASES OF DEAD TRADERS

Hope

There are two times traders use hope, and both times it means they are doing something wrong.

When a trader enters a position and *hopes* it moves in his or her favor, he or she obviously does not have a winning trading plan. A winning trading plan is one in which the historical odds of profitability are in your favor. One does not need hope for this. The edge is already on your side. For example, when one correctly trades undeniables on stock sector indexes, the odds historically state the trade should be profitable more than 70 percent of the time. Hope is not needed, only proper trade execution. Hope is only needed when one enters a trade based on a tip or a gut feeling or some oscillator reading that has never been quantified.

The second time hope comes into play is when a trade is entered and it immediately becomes a loss. Instead of having a predetermined money management plan (a stop), the trader becomes paralyzed (we call this the Bambi syndrome) and *hopes* the loss does not become bigger. This paralysis can last as little as a few minutes to as long as many weeks. Unfortunately, because of the paralysis, the loss can eventually become very large, and the trader gets hurt.

Finally on the rare occasions that hope works, the damage done will be worse. The trader has applied negative behavior (hope, lack of money management, and so on) and is positively reinforced (profit). This will only make it harder in the future for the trader to become successful.

The I-Want-to-Be-Like-Babe-Ruth-When-I-Grow-Up Syndrome

Every trader wants to hit a home run and be a hero among his friends. Everyone loves to hear the stories of the guy who bought soybeans at six cents and liquidated them a few weeks later at 11 cents. In reality, it doesn't quite work that way. For every home run one trader hits, another 50 potential home-run hitters are striking out. Instead of locking into a profit with stops, the home-run hitter is pyramiding his positions. Most times though, his strategy backfires, and his profits are turned into large losses.

The majority of successful traders hit lots of singles, a few doubles and triples, and an occasional home run. The trading strategies in this book are structured to do the same. If you had a choice, would you rather bat .400 hitting lots of singles or bat .200, hit a few home runs, and strike out a lot?

The Playing-with-the-House's-Money-Syndrome

After a string of profitable trades, many traders take the attitude that they can "shoot the works" because they are "playing with the house's money." This is reckless trading and a loser's strategy. When traders get this urge, they should go out and buy some lottery tickets because the results will be the same—a loss. If their attitude were that they were playing with their children's education money, the urge to go for broke would be less likely.

The Friedrich-Nietzsche Syndrome

Most men are raised to believe that pain is synonymous with manhood and strength. In sports, "sucking it up" is encouraged. As sports participants, we accept this principle. As traders, we don't. Losses cause pain. The larger the loss, the more the pain. The more pain one has, the more money one is losing. Friedrich Nietzsche's sentiment, "That which does not kill me makes me stronger," may be true in some aspects of life but is quite untrue when it comes to trading.

THE CURE FOR TRADING DISEASES: STOPS

Stop orders must become traders' and investors' best friend. Stops must become the most important part of the trading program. The moment an order is filled, a protective stop must be placed. The original stop used should reflect the amount the trader is willing to lose, or it must be placed at a strategic trading position. Most successful futures traders risk 1–3 percent of their total capital in a position. Successful equity traders are usually willing to risk a slightly larger amount.

After a position begins moving in a profitable direction, the stop should be adjusted to lock into the profit. For example, if one buys a stock at 20, a stop can be placed at 18 1/2. If the stock rallies to 22, the stop can be moved to above 20 to lock into a small profit. As the stock moves higher, the stop should move higher. This allows the trader to maximize the price profit potential of the position.

Do we sometimes get stopped out of a position only to see the market reverse and the original move continue? Of course, but this is part of the game. We would rather get stopped out than run the risk of ruin by having a position move drastically against us.

Finally, in case you decide to apply this money-management philosophy to your trading, you will be in good company. We will end this chapter with a few quotes from *Market Wizards* by some of the best traders in the world:

Risk control is the most important thing in trading. If I have a position going against me, I get right out.

Paul Tudor Jones

I try very hard not to risk more than 1 percent of my portfolio on any single trade.

Bruce Kovnar

The first rule we live by is never risk more than 1 percent of total equity on any trade.

Larry Hite

Know your "uncle point" and honor it. I have a pain threshold and if I reach that point I must get out.

Marty Schwartz

The elements of good trading are:
1. Cutting losses.
2. Cutting losses.
3. Cutting losses.
If you follow these three rules you may have a chance.

Ed Seykota

Chapter Eight

-
-
-
-
-

Survival of the Fittest

My goal is to be recognized as the best.
When they say middle linebacker from now on,
I want them to mean Butkus.

Dick Butkus

Trading is a tough game. In the futures markets, 97 percent of all traders lose. Those who win, win big. Individuals such as George Soros, Monroe Trout, and Bruce Kovner make millions year in and year out. Those millions do not appear from the sky. They are taken from the pockets of the 97 percent who lose.

What do the 3 percent have that the other 97 percent don't have? A trading methodology combined with proper money management and a proper psychology that works.

We believe that in order to survive and prosper at the trading game one must develop a "survival of the fittest" mindset. We believe the four most important components of that mindset are commitment, a daily approach that is different from the herd, an unshakable belief system, and guts.

COMMITMENT

If you think succeeding at trading is easy, you are out of your mind. Unless you are fully committed to this game, you will lose. Commitment doesn't mean studying the markets when you feel up to it or when you find the time. It means studying them seven days a week.

Success in trading is no different than success in anything else. Dan Gable worked out twice a day, seven days a week, for six years in his quest to win an Olympic gold medal in wrestling. During the football season, Vince Lombardi worked 18 hours a day and slept in his office most nights. Hedge fund manager Mark Strome, whose fund appreciated over 130 percent in 1993, reportedly works 14 hours a day, seven days a week. Marty Schwartz said in *Market Wizards* that he worked 15 hours a day. Imagine attempting to wrestle Dan Gable or coach against Vince Lombardi by working a few hours a week. It would be insane, yet that is what the majority of people do when they attempt to enter the trading arena and compete against the likes of Strome and Schwartz.

Unless you are willing to commit yourself to this game with drive, determination, desire, and persistence, you will always be part of the 97 percent of the traders who lose.

A DAILY APPROACH THAT IS DIFFERENT FROM THE HERD

The average trader/investor doesn't have a daily plan of attack. Instead, he is a clay pigeon waiting to get shot by an onslaught of outside forces. Instead of having a proven trading methodology that is void of outside interference, he is swayed by anything and everything. His trading plan consists of listening to the last analyst interviewed by CNBC, trading on the advice of the lastest guru quoted by *The Wall Street Journal*, investing in his broker's pick of the day, or plunging on the recommendation of a newsletter he subscribes to. Instead of waiting for the correct moment to trade a historically proven strategy, he will jump into the fracas and let the chips fall where they may.

Successful traders have a daily plan that works consistently over a period of time. Their trading methodologies work in bull markets, bear markets, and sideways markets. Their trading methodologies exploit periods of high volatility as well as low volatility. If their methods don't make money in certain markets, they avoid those markets.

Successful traders are not swayed by analysts on television, analysts in newspapers, brokers with stories, or gurus who sell newsletters. Successful traders have the war won before ever fighting a battle. Losing traders do not!

AN UNSHAKABLE BELIEF SYSTEM

We said above that most successful traders have won the war before the first battle is fought. This is a critical concept in trading. There is enormous peace of mind in knowing you have a trading methodology that consistently makes money in the markets. Unfortunately, few people ever achieve this peace of mind.

To truly achieve success at trading, you must have an unshakable belief in your trading plan. You must know that the odds are in your favor. The only way to achieve this belief is by actually trading your system in the real markets and experiencing the ups and downs that accompany all plans. Your plan of attack doesn't have to be identical to ours. There are plenty of other strategies that work. The main thing is for you to be totally comfortable with your approach and to understand that there will be times when losses occur.

The confidence we have in our plan comes from us knowing three things: 1) the results achieved from back-testing our strategies, 2) the results achieved from actual trading, and 3) the knowledge that we can always make our strategies better. Again, our methodology is not the only methodology that works, but it does work for us. We have an enormous amount of faith in our plan. We honestly believe we can make money every month of the year with our strategies. Of course there will be periods of drawdowns, but overall our belief in the plan allows us to withstand this. Finally, and most importantly, our belief allows us to ignore the constant bombardment of outside investment advice, much of which has never been properly tested or quantified.

GUTS

It takes guts to be different from the crowd. We are all essentially social creatures who find solace in being part of the crowd. Unfortunately, successful trading means going against the herd.

News reversals are one of our most profitable strategies, yet psychologically they are the toughest for most investors to trade. Take the example from Chapter 2 of the day after the November 1994 elections. While everyone is screaming "buy, buy, buy," you have to be on the sidelines waiting patiently for the market to reverse. Not only are you not participating in all the initial excitement, but should the market reverse, as it did that day, you will be profiting at the expense of others. For many traders, this is an extremely difficult situation, yet this is why this strategy is so successful.

Let us also look at the other trading chapters. With CHADTP, you will be buying in the face of negative events, and you will be selling in the face of positive events. The same is true for undeniables. You are selling shortly after an index sector makes short-term highs and buying shortly after an index sector makes new lows. In all three reversal strategies, you will be the lone wolf; there will be an enormous amount of outside noise you will need to ignore in order to successfully implement these trades.

The historical volatility strategy is a bit different, but the concept is the same. While the markets are going through periods of indecision and complacency, you will be the lonely individual waiting for an explosion to occur. By ignoring the complacency, you will have the advantage of entering a position far earlier than the other participants. Many times, the explosion will occur, apparently for no reason. Analysts will talk of the lack of fundamental reasons for the move and potential false breakouts, but you will know better.

Finally, your money-management strategy is different from most other traders. While others are waiting for the fundamentals to play themselves out (a nice way of saying the position is moving against them), you are a vigilante with your stops. While other are looking for 100 percent moves, you are a realist and looking for 2–4 percent moves. While others plunge recklessly, you patiently wait until the odds are in your favor.

All combined, this mindset requires an enormous amount of self-discipline. This discipline, though, can and will be rewarded when harnessed properly. Remember, if it was easy, everyone would be doing it.

Finally, we end this chapter by quoting a plaque that hangs in our office.

WHAT IT TAKES TO BE NO. 1

Winning is not a sometime thing; it's an all the time thing. You don't win once in a while; you don't do things right once in a while; you do them right all the time. Winning is a habit. Unfortunately, so is losing.

There is no room for second place. There is only one place in my game, and that's first place. I have finished second twice in my time at Green Bay, and I don't ever want to finish second again. There is a second place bowl game, but it is a game for losers played by losers. It is and always has been an American zeal to be first in anything we do, and to win, and to win, and to win.

Every time a football player goes to ply his trade, he's got to play from the ground up—from the soles of his feet right up to his head. Every inch of him has to play. Some guys play with their heads. That's O.K. You've got to be smart to be number one in any business. But more importantly, you've got to play with your heart, with every fiber of you body. If you're lucky enough to find a guy with a lot of head and a lot of heart, he's never going to come off the field second.

Running a football team is no different than running any other kind of organization—an army, political party or a business. The principles are the same. The object is to win—to beat the other guy. Maybe that sounds hard or cruel. I don't think it is.

It is a reality of life that men are competitive and the most competitive games draw the most competitive men. That's why they are there—to compete. To know the rules and objectives when they get in the game. The object is to win fairly, squarely, by the rules—but to win.

And in truth, I've never known a man worth his salt who in the long run, deep down in his heart, didn't appreciate the grind, the discipline. There is something in good men that really yearns for discipline and the harsh reality of head to head combat.

I don't say these things because I believe in the "brute" nature of man or that men must be brutalized to be combative. I believe in God, and I believe in human decency. But I firmly believe that any man's finest hour—his greatest fulfillment to all he holds dear—is that moment when he has to work his heart out in a good cause and he's exhausted on the field of battle—victorious.

Vince Lombardi

Chapter Nine

-
-
-
-
-

Putting It All Together

Everyone has the will to win,
but few have the will to prepare to win.

Bobby Knight

Where do you go from here? There are two approaches. The first approach says you trade one or two of the strategies in this book when you see fit. Most people do not have the time nor the inclination to trade more than that. The second approach says you give an all-out 100 percent effort to apply the concepts in this book and attempt to master the markets.

How is this done? First, you must make the commitment needed to win at this game. A commitment means studying the behavior of the markets every day. Put yourself on a study program. Use your computer to test historical data. Do this until you have 100 percent confidence in your strategies. Make sure these strategies include good money-management techniques. Why go through all the effort, only to wipe yourself out on one loss?

Each evening, calculate the numbers for CHADTP, VIX, NDX-SPX, and historical volatility. List the possible news reversals and undeniables. (See the example of a sample trade sheet at the end of this chapter.) Do this until it becomes a habit.

Try to improve upon the strategies in this book. This book gives you the basis to become a very *good* trader. There are plenty of additional strategies that can help you become a *great* trader. Spend some time with the trade summaries for CHADTP and NDX-SPX. Attempt to look at each trade individually. How would you trade each situation? Could you make each situation more profitable? Also, in the appendix, is information on additional research reports we have written and books and courses we recommend to make you a better trader.

We would like to end this book with a comment on our trading approach. Many people feel that no trading strategy works all the time. We respect that opinion, yet we disagree. Markets are made up of human begins with emotions. These emotions are innate and are a permanent part of the decision-making process that makes up market price. Markets will always become overbought and oversold. Markets will always range from periods of high volatility to periods of low volatility. Human emotions will continue to become irrational at these extreme points. We firmly believe any proven strategy that can exploit these emotions will stand the test of time.

A Possible Daily Trade Sheet Based on the Strategies Presented in This Book

9/26/94

Indicators	Signal	Action
CHADTP	-608.60	Buy at 464.30
VIX	14.49	No trade
SPX/NDX	-1.75	Sell on opening
Fair Value	3.23	

Undeniables	Trigger Signal	Action
CBOE Biotech Index (BGX)	108.42(L) -1 tick	Sell 110 calls
CBOE Israel Index (ISX)	196.99(L) -1 tick	Sell 195 calls
AMEX Computer Index (XCI)	149.76(L) -1 tick	Sell 150 calls
Phila Utility Index (UTY)	213.78(H) +1 tick	Sell 215 puts
S&P Health Care Index (HCX)	196.99(L) -1 tick	Sell 195 calls

Historical Volatility
(Possible Trades)

DMZ4
SFZ4
Ford (F)
Toys R Us (TOY)
William Co. (WMB)

Potential News Reversals

Date	Event
9/23	Wheat: Large sale to Egypt

-
-
-
-
-

Reading List

We have read over 500 books on trading and investing over the years. The following are among the best of the best.

Boucher, Mark

Turning the Art of Trading Into a Science
Finding Explosive Opportunities In Any Market Environment

We purchased Mark's course, *Turning the Art of Trading Into a Science,* in 1991, and found it to be one of the best investments we ever made. Shortly thereafter, we asked Mark to test a trading program for us. We found his work, like his course, to be meticulous. Mark is not only a maverick in the research arena, he is also a superb money manager. Available through Investment Research Associates 415–967–2213.

Caplan, David

The Options Advantage: Gaining a Trading Edge Over the Markets
The Option Secret
Opportunities In Options newsletter

We rank these books and newsletter among the best in the industry. Dave is a pioneer in the application of option volatility and has built a thriving trading and brokerage operation based on these strategies. His books and newsletters are a must for all option traders. Available through Opportunities In Options, Inc. 310–456–9699. We have arranged to have a free newsletter sent to anyone who inquires.

Connors, Laurence and Blake Hayward

Trading News Reversals and Non-News Reversals
Successful Day Trading Strategies for the Futures Markets
Historical Volatility: An in-depth study

These reports and studies were originally published for a private investment partnership. Contact Robert Arciniaga about their availability c/o Oceanview Financial Research, Inc., 6243 Tapia Drive, Malibu, CA 90265, 800-797-2584.

Crabel, Toby

Day Trading With Short-Term Price Patterns and Opening Range Breakout

We have spent literally hundreds of hours researching this book's concepts. This is one of those rare books that quantifies price persistency for short-term traders. The research is thorough; the trading possibilities are unending. Also recommended by Linda Bradford Rashke of *Market Wizards* fame. Available through Traders Press 800–927–8222.

Natenberg, Sheldon

Option Volatility and Pricing, 2nd Edition

This book should be read and reread by every serious option trader. Every time we open this book, we learn something new. Combine this book with Caplan's books for a total mastery of the options market. Available through Probus Publishing 800–634-3966.

Ross, Joe

Trading by the Minute
Trading by the Book

Probably two of the best books available for individuals aspiring to become professional traders. A wealth of information, with plenty of examples to learn from. Joe's concepts are among the best in the business. Available through Trading Educators 809–373–7436.

Schwager, Jack

Market Wizards
The New Market Wizards

You can tell how we feel about these two books from the number of times we refer to them. A must for everyone. Available in most bookstores.

Soros, George

Alchemy of Finance

The person every hedge fund manager tries to emulate. The insight one gains from this book is invaluable. Available in most bookstores.

Appendix

-
-
-
-
-

HISTORICAL VOLATILITY CALCULATIONS

The historical volatility is defined as the standard deviation of the logarithmic price changes measured at regular intervals of time. Since settlement prices are usually considered the most reliable, the most common method of computing volatility involves using settlement-to-settlement price changes. We defined each price change (x_i) as:

$$x_i = \ln\left(\frac{P_i}{P_{i-1}}\right)$$

where P_i is the price of the underlying contract at the end of the ith time interval, P_i/P_{i-1} is sometimes referred to as the *price relative.*

Week	Underlying Price	$\ln(P_i/P_{i-1})$	Mean	Deviation from Mean	Deviation Squared
0	101.35				
1	102.26	+.008939		.007771	.000060
2	99.07	−.031692		−.032859	.001080
3	100.39	+.013236		.012069	.000146
4	100.76	+.003679		.002512	.000006
5	103.59	+.027699	+.0011167	.026532	.000704
6	99.26	−.042698		−.043865	.001924
7	98.28	−.009922		−.011089	.000123
8	99.98	+.017150		.015982	.000255
9	103.78	+.037303		.036136	.001306
10	102.54	<u>−.012020</u>		−.013188	<u>.000174</u>
		+.011674			.005778

We first calculate the standard deviation of the logarithmic price changes:

$$\text{standard deviation} \quad = \sqrt{(.005778/9)}$$
$$= \sqrt{.000642}$$
$$= .025338$$

We then calculate the annual volatility by multiplying the standard deviation by the square root of the time interval between price changes. Since we looked at price changes every week, the time interval is 365/7:

$$\text{annualized volatility} \quad = .025338 \times \sqrt{(365/7)}$$
$$= .025338 \times \sqrt{52.14}$$
$$= .025338 \times 7.22$$
$$= .1829 \ (18.29\%)$$

Reprinted from:

Option Volatility & Pricing, Advanced Trading Strategies and Techniques, 2nd edition

By Sheldon Natenberg
Probus Publishing Company
1333 Burr Ridge
Burr Ridge, IL 60521

INDICES WITH OPTIONS

- 5-Year Yield Index (FVX)

- 10-Year Yield Index (TNX)

- 30-Year Yield Index (TYX)

- AMEX Biotech Index (BTK)

- AMEX Computer Technology Index (XCI)

- AMEX Hong Kong 30 Option Index (HKO)

- AMEX Japan Index (JPN)

- AMEX Major Market Leaps Index (XLT)

- AMEX Mexico Index (MXY)

- AMEX Natural Gas Index (XNG)

- AMEX North American Telecommunications Index (XTC)

- AMEX Oil Index (XOI)

- AMEX Pharmaceutical Index (DRG)

- CBOE Biotech Index (BGX)

- CBOE Computer Software Index (CWX)

- CBOE Environmental Index (EVX)

- CBOE Financial Times-Stock Exchange 100 Index (FTSX)

- CBOE Gaming Index (GAX)

- CBOE Israel Index (ISX)

- CBOE Russell 2000 Index (RUY)

- CBOE Telecommunications Index (TCX)

- Morgan Stanley Consumer Index (CMR)

- Morgan Stanley Cyclical Index (CYC)

- NASDAQ 100 Index (NDX)

- Philadelphia Gold & Silver Index (XAU)

- Philadelphia National OTC Index (XOC)
- Philadelphia Phone Sector Index (PNX)
- Philadelphia Semiconductor Index (SOX)
- Philadelphia Utility Index (UTY)
- Philadelphia/KBW Bank Index (BKX)
- S&P Banking Index (BIX)
- S&P Chemical Index (CEX)
- S&P Health Care Index (HCX)
- S&P Retail Index (RELX)
- S&P Transportation Index (TRX)
- Short Term Interest Rate Index (IRX)

NDX-SPX Dow Jones Industrial Average Trade Summary

NDX–SPX *DWI X S–Daily 01/02/91–11/30/94

Date	Time	Type	Cnts	Price	Signal Name	Entry P/L*	Cumulative*
01/04/91		Buy	1	2574.26			
01/14/91		LExit	1	2464.60		−109.66	−109.66
01/14/91		Sell	1	2464.60			
01/15/91		SExit	1	2485.64		−21.04	−130.70
01/15/91		Buy	1	2485.64			
01/18/91		LExit	1	2611.14		125.50	−5.20
01/18/91		Sell	1	2611.14			
01/22/91		SExit	1	2625.74		−14.60	−19.80
01/22/91		Buy	1	2625.74			
01/25/91		LExit	1	2645.05		19.31	−0.49
01/25/91		Sell	1	2645.05			
01/29/91		SExit	1	2648.51		−3.46	--3.95
01/29/91		Buy	1	2648.51			
01/31/91		LExit	1	2706.19		57.68	53.73
01/31/91		Sell	1	2706.19			
02/01/91		SExit	1	2735.15		−28.96	24.77
02/01/91		Buy	1	2735.15			
02/05/91		LExit	1	2769.55		34.40	59.17
02/05/91		Sell	1	2769.55			
02/06/91		SExit	1	2773.51		−3.96	55.21
02/06/91		Buy	1	2773.51			
02/07/91		LExit	1	2831.68		58.17	113.38
02/07/91		Sell	1	2831.68			
02/13/91		SExit	1	2867.57		−35.89	77.49
02/13/91		Buy	1	2867.57			
02/14/91		LExit	1	2914.85		47.28	124.77
02/14/91		Sell	1	2914.85			
02/15/91		SExit	1	2881.68		33.17	157.94
02/15/91		Buy	1	2881.68			
02/19/91		LExit	1	2924.75		43.07	201.01
02/19/91		Sell	1	2924.75			

* In Dow Jones Industrial points, not dollars.

NDX–SPX *DWI X S–Daily 01/02/91–11/30/94

Date	Time	Type	Cnts	Price	Signal Name	Entry P/L*	Cumulative*
02/20/91		SExit	1	2909.16		15.59	216.60
02/20/91		Buy	1	2909.16			
02/22/91		LExit	1	2888.12		−21.04	195.56
02/22/91		Sell	1	2888.12			
02/25/91		SExit	1	2924.01		−35.89	159.67
02/25/91		Buy	1	2924.01			
02/26/91		LExit	1	2866.83		−57.18	102.49
02/26/91		Sell	1	2866.83			
02/27/91		SExit	1	2868.07		−1.24	101.25
02/27/91		Buy	1	2868.07			
02/28/91		LExit	1	2910.64		42.57	143.82
02/28/91		Sell	1	2910.64			
03/01/91		SExit	1	2859.65		50.99	194.81
03/01/91		Buy	1	2859.65			
03/04/91		LExit	1	2924.50		64.85	259.66
03/04/91		Sell	1	2924.50			
03/05/91		SExit	1	2925.50		−1.00	258.66
03/05/91		Buy	1	2925.50			
03/11/91		LExit	1	2952.97		27.47	286.13
03/11/91		Sell	1	2952.97			
03/14/91		SExit	1	2965.35		−12.38	273.75
03/14/91		Buy	1	2965.35			
03/15/91		LExit	1	2956.44		−8.91	264.84
03/15/91		Sell	1	2956.44			
03/19/91		SExit	1	2881.44		75.00	339.84
03/19/91		Buy	1	2881.44			
03/22/91		LExit	1	2846.29		−35.15	304.69
03/22/91		Sell	1	2846.29			
03/26/91		SExit	1	2859.90		−13.61	291.08
03/26/91		Buy	1	2859.90			
04/01/91		LExit	1	2901.98		42.08	333.16
04/01/91		Sell	1	2901.98			
04/02/91		SExit	1	2893.32		8.66	341.82

* In Dow Jones Industrial points, not dollars.

NDX–SPX *DWI X S–Daily 01/02/91–11/30/94

Date	Time	Type	Cnts	Price	Signal Name	Entry P/L*	Cumulative*
04/02/91		Buy	1	2893.32			
04/09/91		LExit	1	2908.42		15.10	356.92
04/09/91		Sell	1	2908.42			
04/10/91		SExit	1	2878.47		29.95	386.87
04/10/91		Buy	1	2878.47			
04/11/91		LExit	1	2895.79		17.32	404.19
04/11/91		Sell	1	2895.79			
04/12/91		SExit	1	2927.97		−32.18	372.01
04/12/91		Buy	1	2927.97			
04/15/91		LExit	1	2926.24		−1.73	370.28
04/15/91		Sell	1	2926.24			
04/22/91		SExit	1	2948.27		−22.03	348.25
04/22/91		Buy	1	2948.27			
04/29/91		LExit	1	2914.85		−33.42	314.83
04/29/91		Sell	1	2914.85			
04/30/91		SExit	1	2887.13		27.72	342.55
04/30/91		Buy	1	2887.13			
05/01/91		LExit	1	2901.49		14.36	356.91
05/01/91		Sell	1	2901.49			
05/03/91		SExit	1	2932.43		−30.94	325.97
05/03/91		Buy	1	2932.43			
05/09/91		LExit	1	2939.40		6.97	332.94
05/09/91		Sell	1	2939.40			
05/13/91		SExit	1	2930.01		9.39	342.33
05/13/91		Buy	1	2930.01			
05/14/91		LExit	1	2913.24		−16.77	325.56
05/14/91		Sell	1	2913.24			
05/15/91		SExit	1	2885.96		27.28	352.84
05/15/91		Buy	1	2885.96			
05/16/91		LExit	1	2882.16		−3.80	349.04
05/16/91		Sell	1	2882.16			
05/23/91		SExit	1	2912.34		−30.18	318.86
05/23/91		Buy	1	2912.34			

* In Dow Jones Industrial points, not dollars.

NDX–SPX *DWI X S–Daily 01/02/91–11/30/94

Date	Time	Type	Cnts	Price	Signal Name	Entry P/L*	Cumulative*
05/28/91		LExit	1	2924.42		12.08	330.94
05/28/91		Sell	1	2924.42			
05/30/91		SExit	1	2965.56		−41.14	289.80
05/30/91		Buy	1	2965.56			
05/31/91		LExit	1	3005.81		40.25	330.05
05/31/91		Sell	1	3005.81			
06/04/91		SExit	1	3006.93		−1.12	328.93
06/04/91		Buy	1	3006.93			
06/06/91		LExit	1	3002.68		−4.25	324.68
06/06/91		Sell	1	3002.68			
06/10/91		SExit	1	2975.63		27.05	351.73
06/10/91		Buy	1	2975.63			
06/11/91		LExit	1	2980.32		4.69	356.42
06/11/91		Sell	1	2980.32			
06/13/91		SExit	1	2962.21		18.11	374.53
06/13/91		Buy	1	2962.21			
06/14/91		LExit	1	2978.31		16.10	390.63
06/14/91		Sell	1	2978.31			
06/18/91		SExit	1	2993.07		−14.76	375.87
06/18/91		Buy	1	2993.07			
06/19/91		LExit	1	2965.34		−27.73	348.14
06/19/91		Sell	1	2965.34			
06/26/91		SExit	1	2908.54		56.80	404.94
06/26/91		Buy	1	2908.54			
07/02/91		LExit	1	2954.38		45.84	450.78
07/02/91		Sell	1	2954.38			
07/05/91		SExit	1	2923.30		31.08	481.86
07/05/91		Buy	1	2923.30			
07/08/91		LExit	1	2909.21		−14.09	467.77
07/08/91		Sell	1	2909.21			
07/09/91		SExit	1	2964.45		−55.24	412.53
07/09/91		Buy	1	2964.45			
07/12/91		LExit	1	2975.40		10.95	423.48

* In Dow Jones Industrial points, not dollars.

NDX–SPX *DWI X S–Daily 01/02/91–11/30/94

Date	Time	Type	Cnts	Price	Signal Name	Entry P/L*	Cumulative*
07/12/91		Sell	1	2975.40			
07/15/91		SExit	1	2980.99		−5.59	417.89
07/15/91		Buy	1	2980.99			
07/16/91		LExit	1	2994.63		13.64	431.53
07/16/91		Sell	1	2994.63			
07/22/91		SExit	1	3014.31		−19.68	411.85
07/22/91		Buy	1	3014.31			
07/23/91		LExit	1	3021.24		6.93	418.78
07/23/91		Sell	1	3021.24			
07/26/91		SExit	1	2976.52		44.72	463.50
07/26/91		Buy	1	2976.52			
07/30/91		LExit	1	2998.88		22.36	485.86
07/30/91		Sell	1	2998.88			
07/31/91		SExit	1	3017.22		−18.34	467.52
07/31/91		Buy	1	3017.22			
08/06/91		LExit	1	2987.48		−29.74	437.78
08/06/91		Sell	1	2987.48			
08/08/91		SExit	1	3024.15		−36.67	401.11
08/08/91		Buy	1	3024.15			
08/16/91		LExit	1	3000.45		−23.70	377.41
08/16/91		Sell	1	3000.45			
08/19/91		SExit	1	2851.97		148.48	525.89
08/19/91		Buy	1	2851.97			
08/21/91		LExit	1	2962.21		110.24	636.13
08/21/91		Sell	1	2962.21			
08/22/91		SExit	1	3017.67		−55.46	580.67
08/22/91		Buy	1	3017.67			
08/23/91		LExit	1	3004.70		−12.97	567.70
08/23/91		Sell	1	3004.70			
08/27/91		SExit	1	3038.91		−34.21	533.49
08/27/91		Buy	1	3038.91			
08/29/91		LExit	1	3057.69		18.78	552.27
08/29/91		Sell	1	3057.69			

* In Dow Jones Industrial points, not dollars.

NDX–SPX *DWI X S–Daily 01/02/91–11/30/94

Date	Time	Type	Cnts	Price	Signal Name	Entry P/L*	Cumulative*
09/04/91		SExit	1	3022.58		35.11	587.38
09/04/91		Buy	1	3022.58			
09/05/91		LExit	1	3013.19		−9.39	577.99
09/05/91		Sell	1	3013.19			
09/10/91		SExit	1	3008.50		4.69	582.68
09/10/91		Buy	1	3008.50			
09/11/91		LExit	1	2989.04		−19.46	563.22
09/11/91		Sell	1	2989.04			
09/12/91		SExit	1	3001.12		−12.08	551.14
09/12/91		Buy	1	3001.12			
09/17/91		LExit	1	3004.03		2.91	554.05
09/17/91		Sell	1	3004.03			
09/19/91		SExit	1	3018.11		−14.08	539.97
09/19/91		Buy	1	3018.11			
09/27/91		LExit	1	3017.22		−0.89	539.08
09/27/91		Sell	1	3017.22			
10/07/91		SExit	1	2959.53		57.69	596.77
10/07/91		Buy	1	2959.53			
10/09/91		LExit	1	2960.42		0.89	597.66
10/09/91		Sell	1	2960.42			
10/10/91		SExit	1	2952.37		8.05	605.71
10/10/91		Buy	1	2952.37			
10/11/91		LExit	1	2983.68		31.31	637.02
10/11/91		Sell	1	2983.68			
10/14/91		SExit	1	2983.68		0.00	637.02
10/14/91		Buy	1	2983.68			
10/18/91		LExit	1	3057.47		73.79	710.81
10/18/91		Sell	1	3057.47			
10/21/91		SExit	1	3077.37		−19.90	690.91
10/21/91		Buy	1	3077.37			
10/24/91		LExit	1	3032.42		−44.95	645.96
10/24/91		Sell	1	3032.42			
10/30/91		SExit	1	3060.38		−27.96	618.00

* In Dow Jones Industrial points, not dollars.

NDX–SPX *DWI X S–Daily 01/02/91–11/30/94

Date	Time	Type	Cnts	Price	Signal Name	Entry P/L*	Cumulative*
10/30/91		Buy	1	3060.38			
11/01/91		LExit	1	3075.36		14.98	632.98
11/01/91		Sell	1	3075.36			
11/06/91		SExit	1	3034.21		41.15	674.13
11/06/91		Buy	1	3034.21			
11/07/91		LExit	1	3039.13		4.92	679.05
11/07/91		Sell	1	3039.13			
11/11/91		SExit	1	3042.04		−2.91	676.14
11/11/91		Buy	1	3042.04			
11/15/91		LExit	1	3058.59		16.55	692.69
11/15/91		Sell	1	3058.59			
11/19/91		SExit	1	2950.36		108.23	800.92
11/19/91		Buy	1	2950.36			
11/26/91		LExit	1	2915.25		−35.11	765.81
11/26/91		Sell	1	2915.25			
11/29/91		SExit	1	2895.13		20.12	785.93
11/29/91		Buy	1	2895.13			
12/12/91		LExit	1	2881.93		−13.20	772.73
12/12/91		Sell	1	2881.93			
12/16/91		SExit	1	2916.59		−34.66	738.07
12/16/91		Buy	1	2916.59			
12/18/91		LExit	1	2894.45		−22.14	715.93
12/18/91		Sell	1	2894.45			
12/26/91		SExit	1	3051.88		−157.43	558.50
12/26/91		Buy	1	3051.88			
01/06/92		LExit	1	3194.10		142.22	700.72
01/06/92		Sell	1	3194.10			
01/07/92		SExit	1	3184.48		9.62	710.34
01/07/92		Buy	1	3184.48			
01/15/92		LExit	1	3257.16		72.68	783.02
01/15/92		Sell	1	3257.16			
01/16/92		SExit	1	3248.66		8.50	791.52
01/16/92		Buy	1	3248.66			

* In Dow Jones Industrial points, not dollars.

NDX–SPX *DWI X S–Daily 01/02/91–11/30/94

Date	Time	Type	Cnts	Price	Signal Name	Entry P/L*	Cumulative*
01/17/92		LExit	1	3250.67		2.01	793.53
01/17/92		Sell	1	3250.67			
01/23/92		SExit	1	3249.33		1.34	794.87
01/23/92		Buy	1	3249.33			
01/27/92		LExit	1	3241.06		−8.27	786.60
01/27/92		Sell	1	3241.06			
01/29/92		SExit	1	3257.38		−16.32	770.28
01/29/92		Buy	1	3257.38			
02/03/92		LExit	1	3219.81		−37.57	732.71
02/03/92		Sell	1	3219.81			
02/04/92		SExit	1	3233.68		−13.87	718.84
02/04/92		Buy	1	3233.68			
02/07/92		LExit	1	3263.19		29.51	748.35
02/07/92		Sell	1	3263.19			
02/10/92		SExit	1	3230.77		32.42	780.77
02/10/92		Buy	1	3230.77			
02/11/92		LExit	1	3246.20		15.43	796.20
02/11/92		Sell	1	3246.20			
02/13/92		SExit	1	3274.15		−27.95	768.25
02/13/92		Buy	1	3274.15			
02/14/92		LExit	1	3226.30		−47.85	720.40
02/14/92		Sell	1	3226.30			
02/21/92		SExit	1	3267.67		−41.37	679.03
02/21/92		Buy	1	3267.67			
02/24/92		LExit	1	3277.50		9.83	688.86
02/24/92		Sell	1	3277.50			
02/26/92		SExit	1	3261.63		15.87	704.73
02/26/92		Buy	1	3261.63			
02/27/92		LExit	1	3280.64		19.01	723.74
02/27/92		Sell	1	3280.64			
02/28/92		SExit	1	3280.64		0.00	723.74
02/28/92		Buy	1	3280.64			
03/02/92		LExit	1	3270.80		−9.84	713.90

* In Dow Jones Industrial points, not dollars.

NDX–SPX *DWI X S–Daily 01/02/91–11/30/94

Date	Time	Type	Cnts	Price	Signal Name	Entry P/L*	Cumulative*
03/02/92		Sell	1	3270.80			
03/03/92		SExit	1	3287.57		−16.77	697.13
03/03/92		Buy	1	3287.57			
03/04/92		LExit	1	3299.19		11.62	708.75
03/04/92		Sell	1	3299.19			
03/11/92		SExit	1	3225.63		73.56	782.31
03/11/92		Buy	1	3225.63			
03/12/92		LExit	1	3207.07		−18.56	763.75
03/12/92		Sell	1	3207.07			
03/17/92		SExit	1	3236.81		−29.74	734.01
03/17/92		Buy	1	3236.81			
03/20/92		LExit	1	3268.78		31.97	765.98
03/20/92		Sell	1	3268.78			
03/26/92		SExit	1	3271.47		−2.69	763.29
03/26/92		Buy	1	3271.47			
03/27/92		LExit	1	3257.83		−13.64	749.65
03/27/92		Sell	1	3257.83			
04/01/92		SExit	1	3220.04		37.79	787.44
04/01/92		Buy	1	3220.04			
04/03/92		LExit	1	3230.55		10.51	797.95
04/03/92		Sell	1	3230.55			
04/07/92		SExit	1	3283.32		−52.77	745.18
04/07/92		Buy	1	3283.32			
04/08/92		LExit	1	3194.99		−88.33	656.85
04/08/92		Sell	1	3194.99			
04/09/92		SExit	1	3193.43		1.56	658.41
04/09/92		Buy	1	3193.43			
04/13/92		LExit	1	3254.70		61.27	719.68
04/13/92		Sell	1	3254.70			
04/14/92		SExit	1	3283.54		−28.84	690.84
04/14/92		Buy	1	3283.54			
04/15/92		LExit	1	3328.26		44.72	735.56
04/15/92		Sell	1	3328.26			

* In Dow Jones Industrial points, not dollars.

NDX–SPX *DWI X S–Daily 01/02/91–11/30/94

Date	Time	Type	Cnts	Price	Signal Name	Entry P/L*	Cumulative*
04/16/92		SExit	1	3352.19		−23.93	711.63
04/16/92		Buy	1	3352.19			
04/20/92		LExit	1	3340.12		−12.07	699.56
04/20/92		Sell	1	3340.12			
04/23/92		SExit	1	3340.12		0.00	699.56
04/23/92		Buy	1	3340.12			
04/24/92		LExit	1	3350.63		10.51	710.07
04/24/92		Sell	1	3350.63			
04/30/92		SExit	1	3332.29		18.34	728.41
04/30/92		Buy	1	3332.29			
05/05/92		LExit	1	3375.45		43.16	771.57
05/05/92		Sell	1	3375.45			
05/06/92		SExit	1	3372.76		2.69	774.26
05/06/92		Buy	1	3372.76			
05/08/92		LExit	1	3372.09		−0.67	773.59
05/08/92		Sell	1	3372.09			
05/13/92		SExit	1	3390.38		−18.29	755.30
05/13/92		Buy	1	3390.38			
05/14/92		LExit	1	3389.01		−1.37	753.93
05/14/92		Sell	1	3389.01			
05/18/92		SExit	1	3369.20		19.81	773.74
05/18/92		Buy	1	3369.20			
05/19/92		LExit	1	3379.69		10.49	784.23
05/19/92		Sell	1	3379.69			
05/21/92		SExit	1	3384.08		−4.39	779.84
05/21/92		Buy	1	3384.08			
05/26/92		LExit	1	3389.62		5.54	785.38
05/26/92		Sell	1	3389.62			
05/27/92		SExit	1	3360.84		28.78	814.16
05/27/92		Buy	1	3360.84			
05/29/92		LExit	1	3405.69		44.85	859.01
05/29/92		Sell	1	3405.69			
06/01/92		SExit	1	3388.58		17.11	876.12

* In Dow Jones Industrial points, not dollars.

NDX–SPX *DWI X S–Daily 01/02/91–11/30/94

Date	Time	Type	Cnts	Price	Signal Name	Entry P/L*	Cumulative*
06/01/92		Buy	1	3388.58			
06/04/92		LExit	1	3408.80		20.22	896.34
06/04/92		Sell	1	3408.80			
06/11/92		SExit	1	3349.18		59.62	955.96
06/11/92		Buy	1	3349.18			
06/12/92		LExit	1	3379.51		30.33	986.29
06/12/92		Sell	1	3379.51			
06/15/92		SExit	1	3339.65		39.86	1026.15
06/15/92		Buy	1	3339.65			
06/16/92		LExit	1	3361.85		22.20	1048.35
06/16/92		Sell	1	3361.85			
06/18/92		SExit	1	3289.90		71.95	1120.30
06/18/92		Buy	1	3289.90			
06/19/92		LExit	1	3282.14		−7.76	1112.54
06/19/92		Sell	1	3282.14			
06/22/92		SExit	1	3278.40		3.74	1116.28
06/22/92		Buy	1	3278.40			
06/23/92		LExit	1	3289.63		11.23	1127.51
06/23/92		Sell	1	3289.63			
06/24/92		SExit	1	3286.69		2.94	1130.45
06/24/92		Buy	1	3286.69			
06/25/92		LExit	1	3298.19		11.50	1141.95
06/25/92		Sell	1	3298.19			
06/30/92		SExit	1	3325.74		−27.55	1114.40
06/30/92		Buy	1	3325.74			
07/06/92		LExit	1	3304.07		−21.67	1092.73
07/06/92		Sell	1	3304.07			
07/09/92		SExit	1	3302.19		1.88	1094.61
07/09/92		Buy	1	3302.19			
07/20/92		LExit	1	3289.50		−12.69	1081.92
07/20/92		Sell	1	3289.50			
07/22/92		SExit	1	3290.04		−0.54	1081.38
07/22/92		Buy	1	3290.04			

* In Dow Jones Industrial points, not dollars.

NDX–SPX *DWI X S–Daily 01/02/91–11/30/94

Date	Time	Type	Cnts	Price	Signal Name	Entry P/L*	Cumulative*
07/23/92		LExit	1	3287.87		−2.17	1079.21
07/23/92		Sell	1	3287.87			
07/24/92		SExit	1	3279.50		8.37	1087.58
07/24/92		Buy	1	3279.50			
07/28/92		LExit	1	3288.95		9.45	1097.03
07/28/92		Sell	1	3288.95			
08/04/92		SExit	1	3392.70		−103.75	993.28
08/04/92		Buy	1	3392.70			
08/05/92		LExit	1	3372.16		−20.54	972.74
08/05/92		Sell	1	3372.16			
08/10/92		SExit	1	3321.91		50.25	1022.99
08/10/92		Buy	1	3321.91			
08/12/92		LExit	1	3327.59		5.68	1028.67
08/12/92		Sell	1	3327.59			
08/14/92		SExit	1	3320.83		6.76	1035.43
08/14/92		Buy	1	3320.83			
08/17/92		LExit	1	3321.37		0.54	1035.97
08/17/92		Sell	1	3321.37			
08/20/92		SExit	1	3313.54		7.83	1043.80
08/20/92		Buy	1	3313.54			
08/24/92		LExit	1	3233.57		−79.97	963.83
08/24/92		Sell	1	3233.57			
08/26/92		SExit	1	3235.19		−1.62	962.21
08/26/92		Buy	1	3235.19			
08/31/92		LExit	1	3273.29		38.10	1000.31
08/31/92		Sell	1	3273.29			
09/01/92		SExit	1	3254.64		18.65	1018.96
09/01/92		Buy	1	3254.64			
09/08/92		LExit	1	3279.23		24.59	1043.55
09/08/92		Sell	1	3279.23			
09/09/92		SExit	1	3261.67		17.56	1061.11
09/09/92		Buy	1	3261.67			
09/17/92		LExit	1	3326.78		65.11	1126.22

* In Dow Jones Industrial points, not dollars.

NDX–SPX *DWI X S–Daily 01/02/91–11/30/94

Date	Time	Type	Cnts	Price	Signal Name	Entry P/L*	Cumulative*
09/17/92		Sell	I	3326.78			
09/18/92		SExit	I	3315.97		10.81	1137.03
09/18/92		Buy	I	3315.97			
09/21/92		LExit	I	3324.62		8.65	1145.68
09/21/92		Sell	I	3324.62			
09/22/92		SExit	I	3315.97		8.65	1154.33
09/22/92		Buy	I	3315.97			
09/28/92		LExit	I	3243.30		−72.67	1081.66
09/28/92		Sell	I	3243.30			
09/30/92		SExit	I	3265.18		−21.88	1059.78
09/30/92		Buy	I	3265.18			
10/02/92		LExit	I	3251.67		−13.51	1046.27
10/02/92		Sell	I	3251.67			
10/05/92		SExit	I	3176.57		75.10	1121.37
10/05/92		Buy	I	3176.57			
10/09/92		LExit	I	3167.65		−8.92	1112.45
10/09/92		Sell	I	3167.65			
10/12/92		SExit	I	3149.01		18.64	1131.09
10/12/92		Buy	I	3149.01			
10/13/92		LExit	I	3177.11		28.10	1159.19
10/13/92		Sell	I	3177.11			
10/14/92		SExit	I	3198.18		−21.07	1138.12
10/14/92		Buy	I	3198.18			
10/15/92		LExit	I	3179.81		−18.37	1119.75
10/15/92		Sell	I	3179.81			
10/16/92		SExit	I	3180.08		−0.27	1119.48
10/16/92		Buy	I	3180.08			
10/27/92		LExit	I	3252.75		72.67	1192.15
10/27/92		Sell	I	3252.75			
10/29/92		SExit	I	3254.10		−1.35	1190.80
10/29/92		Buy	I	3254.10			
11/03/92		LExit	I	3268.69		14.59	1205.39
11/03/92		Sell	I	3268.69			

* In Dow Jones Industrial points, not dollars.

NDX–SPX *DWI X S–Daily 01/02/91–11/30/94

Date	Time	Type	Cnts	Price	Signal Name	Entry P/L*	Cumulative*
11/05/92		SExit	1	3221.68		47.01	1252.40
11/05/92		Buy	1	3221.68			
11/12/92		LExit	1	3245.73		24.05	1276.45
11/12/92		Sell	1	3245.73			
11/16/92		SExit	1	3226.28		19.45	1295.90
11/16/92		Buy	1	3226.28			
11/17/92		LExit	1	3207.92		−18.37	1277.53
11/17/92		Sell	1	3207.91			
11/19/92		SExit	1	3214.12		−6.21	1271.32
11/19/92		Buy	1	3214.12			
11/23/92		LExit	1	3223.31		9.19	1280.51
11/23/92		Sell	1	3223.31			
11/25/92		SExit	1	3255.99		−32.68	1247.83
11/25/92		Buy	1	3255.99			
11/27/92		LExit	1	3272.75		16.76	1264.59
11/27/92		Sell	1	3272.75			
12/01/92		SExit	1	3299.22		−26.47	1238.12
12/01/92		Buy	1	3299.22			
12/03/92		LExit	1	3284.90		−14.32	1223.80
12/03/92		Sell	1	3284.90			
12/04/92		SExit	1	3285.17		−0.27	1223.53
12/04/92		Buy	1	3285.17			
12/09/92		LExit	1	3319.48		34.31	1257.84
12/09/92		Sell	1	3319.48			
12/17/92		SExit	1	3256.81		62.67	1320.51
12/17/92		Buy	1	3256.81			
12/21/92		LExit	1	3304.89		48.08	1368.59
12/21/92		Sell	1	3304.89			
12/22/92		SExit	1	3321.37		−16.48	1352.11
12/22/92		Buy	1	3321.37			
12/23/92		LExit	1	3320.56		−0.81	1351.30
12/23/92		Sell	1	3320.56			
12/24/92		SExit	1	3315.43		5.13	1356.43

* In Dow Jones Industrial points, not dollars.

NDX–SPX *DWI X S–Daily 01/02/91–11/30/94

Date	Time	Type	Cnts	Price	Signal Name	Entry P/L*	Cumulative*
12/24/92		Buy	1	3315.43			
12/31/92		LExit	1	3323.54		8.11	1364.54
12/31/92		Sell	1	3323.54			
01/04/93		SExit	1	3312.46		11.08	1375.62
01/04/93		Buy	1	3312.46			
01/05/93		LExit	1	3306.52		−5.94	1369.68
01/05/93		Sell	1	3306.52			
01/06/93		SExit	1	3303.54		2.98	1372.66
01/06/93		Buy	1	3303.54			
01/13/93		LExit	1	3254.10		−49.44	1323.22
01/13/93		Sell	1	3254.10			
01/14/93		SExit	1	3276.26		−22.16	1301.06
01/14/93		Buy	1	3276.26			
01/18/93		LExit	1	3269.50		−6.76	1294.30
01/18/93		Sell	1	3269.50			
01/21/93		SExit	1	3241.68		27.82	1322.12
01/21/93		Buy	1	3241.68			
01/25/93		LExit	1	3270.04		28.36	1350.48
01/25/93		Sell	1	3270.04			
02/02/93		SExit	1	3322.45		−52.41	1298.07
02/02/93		Buy	1	3222.45			
02/04/93		LExit	1	3398.10		75.65	1373.72
02/04/93		Sell	1	3398.10			
02/11/93		SExit	1	3418.63		−20.53	1353.19
02/11/93		Buy	1	3418.63			
02/12/93		LExit	1	3420.52		1.89	1355.08
02/12/93		Sell	1	3420.52			
02/19/93		SExit	1	3313.27		107.25	1462.33
02/19/93		Buy	1	3313.27			
02/22/93		LExit	1	3321.91		8.64	1470.97
02/22/93		Sell	1	3321.91			
02/24/93		SExit	1	3325.16		−3.25	1467.72
02/24/93		Buy	1	3325.16			

* In Dow Jones Industrial points, not dollars.

NDX–SPX *DWI X S–Daily 01/02/91–11/30/94

Date	Time	Type	Cnts	Price	Signal Name	Entry P/L*	Cumulative*
03/01/93		LExit	1	3380.81		55.65	1523.37
03/01/93		Sell	1	3380.81			
03/03/93		SExit	1	3403.77		−22.96	1500.41
03/03/93		Buy	1	3403.77			
03/05/93		LExit	1	3404.58		0.81	1501.22
03/05/93		Sell	1	3404.58			
03/08/93		SExit	1	3417.82		−13.24	1487.98
03/08/93		Buy	1	3417.82			
03/09/93		LExit	1	3468.07		50.25	1538.23
03/09/93		Sell	1	3468.07			
03/10/93		SExit	1	3470.23		−2.16	1536.07
03/10/93		Buy	1	3470.23			
03/11/93		LExit	1	3472.39		2.16	1538.23
03/11/93		Sell	1	3472.39			
03/12/93		SExit	1	3428.09		44.30	1582.53
03/12/93		Buy	1	3428.09			
03/17/93		LExit	1	3436.19		8.10	1590.63
03/17/93		Sell	1	3436.19			
03/25/93		SExit	1	3446.73		−10.54	1580.09
03/25/93		Buy	1	3446.73			
03/30/93		LExit	1	3455.92		9.19	1589.28
03/30/93		Sell	1	3455.92			
03/31/93		SExit	1	3466.18		−10.26	1579.02
03/31/93		Buy	1	3466.18			
04/02/93		LExit	1	3426.47		−39.71	1539.31
04/02/93		Sell	1	3426.47			
04/06/93		SExit	1	3385.40		41.07	1580.38
04/06/93		Buy	1	3385.40			
04/07/93		LExit	1	3377.03		−8.37	1572.01
04/07/93		Sell	1	3377.03			
04/08/93		SExit	1	3405.93		−28.90	1543.11
04/08/93		Buy	1	3405.93			
04/12/93		LExit	1	3405.66		−0.27	1542.84

* In Dow Jones Industrial points, not dollars.

NDX–SPX *DWI X S–Daily 01/02/91–11/30/94

Date	Time	Type	Cnts	Price	Signal Name	Entry P/L*	Cumulative*
04/12/93		Sell	1	3405.66			
04/13/93		SExit	1	3437.00		−31.34	1511.50
04/13/93		Buy	1	3437.00			
04/14/93		LExit	1	3444.30		7.30	1518.80
04/14/93		Sell	1	3444.30			
04/15/93		SExit	1	3452.40		−8.10	1510.70
04/15/93		Buy	1	3452.40			
04/16/93		LExit	1	3465.10		12.70	1523.40
04/16/93		Sell	1	3465.10			
04/21/93		SExit	1	3446.19		18.91	1542.31
04/21/93		Buy	1	3446.19			
04/26/93		LExit	1	3407.56		−38.63	1503.68
04/26/93		Sell	1	3407.56			
04/28/93		SExit	1	3417.55		−9.99	1493.69
04/28/93		Buy	1	3417.55			
04/30/93		LExit	1	3435.65		18.10	1511.79
04/30/93		Sell	1	3435.65			
05/04/93		SExit	1	3448.89		−13.24	1498.55
05/04/93		Buy	1	3448.89			
05/07/93		LExit	1	3447.16		−1.73	1496.82
05/07/93		Sell	1	3447.16			
05/10/93		SExit	1	3442.18		4.98	1501.80
05/10/93		Buy	1	3442.18			
05/12/93		LExit	1	3462.38		20.20	1522.00
05/12/93		Sell	1	3462.38			
05/14/93		SExit	1	3449.37		13.01	1535.01
05/14/93		Buy	1	3449.37			
05/25/93		LExit	1	3508.61		59.24	1594.25
05/25/93		Sell	1	3508.61			
05/27/93		SExit	1	3553.45		−44.84	1549.41
05/27/93		Buy	1	3553.45			
05/28/93		LExit	1	3546.80		−6.65	1542.76
05/28/93		Sell	1	3546.80			

* In Dow Jones Industrial points, not dollars.

NDX–SPX *DWI X S–Daily 01/02/91–11/30/94

Date	Time	Type	Cnts	Price	Signal Name	Entry P/L*	Cumulative*
06/02/93		SExit	1	3548.74		−1.94	1540.82
06/02/93		Buy	1	3548.74			
06/07/93		LExit	1	3548.46		−0.28	1540.54
06/07/93		Sell	1	3548.46			
06/14/93		SExit	1	3513.31		35.15	1575.69
06/14/93		Buy	1	3513.31			
06/17/93		LExit	1	3511.37		−1.94	1573.75
06/17/93		Sell	1	3511.37			
06/24/93		SExit	1	3467.09		44.28	1618.03
06/24/93		Buy	1	3467.09			
06/25/93		LExit	1	3493.38		26.29	1644.32
06/25/93		Sell	1	3493.38			
06/28/93		SExit	1	3500.58		−7.20	1637.12
06/28/93		Buy	1	3500.58			
06/30/93		LExit	1	3517.46		16.88	1654.00
06/30/93		Sell	1	3517.46			
07/01/93		SExit	1	3520.51		−3.05	1650.95
07/01/93		Buy	1	3520.51			
07/02/93		LExit	1	3497.81		−22.70	1628.25
07/02/93		Sell	1	3497.81			
07/06/93		SExit	1	3489.51		8.30	1636.55
07/06/93		Buy	1	3489.51			
07/08/93		LExit	1	3480.65		−8.86	1627.69
07/08/93		Sell	1	3480.65			
07/12/93		SExit	1	3522.17		−41.52	1586.17
07/12/93		Buy	1	3522.17			
07/13/93		LExit	1	3521.31		−0.86	1585.31
07/13/93		Sell	1	3521.31			
07/14/93		SExit	1	3519.63		1.68	1586.99
07/14/93		Buy	1	3519.63			
07/15/93		LExit	1	3541.43		21.80	1608.79
07/15/93		Sell	1	3541.43			
07/21/93		SExit	1	3538.08		3.35	1612.14

* In Dow Jones Industrial points, not dollars.

NDX–SPX *DWI X S–Daily 01/02/91–11/30/94

Date	Time	Type	Cnts	Price	Signal Name	Entry P/L*	Cumulative*
07/21/93		Buy	1	3538.08			
07/22/93		LExit	1	3553.45		15.37	1627.51
07/22/93		Sell	1	3553.45			
07/26/93		SExit	1	3553.72		−0.27	1627.24
07/26/93		Buy	1	3553.72			
07/28/93		LExit	1	3561.83		8.11	1635.35
07/28/93		Sell	1	3561.83			
07/29/93		SExit	1	3558.20		3.63	1638.98
07/29/93		Buy	1	3558.20			
07/30/93		LExit	1	3566.02		7.82	1646.80
07/30/93		Sell	1	3566.02			
08/03/93		SExit	1	3559.87		6.15	1652.95
08/03/93		Buy	1	3559.87			
08/10/93		LExit	1	3572.17		12.30	1665.25
08/10/93		Sell	1	3572.17			
08/12/93		SExit	1	3595.08		−22.91	1642.34
08/12/93		Buy	1	3595.08			
08/16/93		LExit	1	3564.90		−30.18	1612.16
08/16/93		Sell	1	3564.90			
08/17/93		SExit	1	3586.98		−22.08	1590.08
08/17/93		Buy	1	3586.98			
08/19/93		LExit	1	3605.98		19.00	1609.08
08/19/93		Sell	1	3605.98			
08/23/93		SExit	1	3604.30		1.68	1610.76
08/23/93		Buy	1	3604.30			
08/25/93		LExit	1	3641.47		37.17	1647.93
08/25/93		Sell	1	3641.47			
08/30/93		SExit	1	3641.19		0.28	1648.21
08/30/93		Buy	1	3641.19			
09/07/93		LExit	1	3631.13		−10.06	1638.15
09/07/93		Sell	1	3631.13			
09/09/93		SExit	1	3578.04		53.09	1691.24
09/09/93		Buy	1	3578.04			

* In Dow Jones Industrial points, not dollars.

NDX–SPX *DWI X S–Daily 01/02/91–11/30/94

Date	Time	Type	Cnts	Price	Signal Name	Entry P/L*	Cumulative*
09/13/93		LExit	1	3629.18		51.14	1742.38
09/13/93		Sell	1	3629.18			
09/16/93		SExit	1	3628.62		0.56	1742.94
09/16/93		Buy	1	3628.62			
10/01/93		LExit	1	3557.36		−71.26	1671.68
10/01/93		Sell	1	3557.36			
10/05/93		SExit	1	3585.02		−27.66	1644.02
10/05/93		Buy	1	3585.02			
10/06/93		LExit	1	3585.58		0.56	1644.58
10/06/93		Sell	1	3585.58			
10/11/93		SExit	1	3586.98		−1.40	1643.18
10/11/93		Buy	1	3586.98			
10/12/93		LExit	1	3600.39		13.41	1656.59
10/12/93		Sell	1	3600.39			
10/13/93		SExit	1	3592.01		8.38	1664.97
10/13/93		Buy	1	3592.01			
10/18/93		LExit	1	3623.87		31.86	1696.83
10/18/93		Sell	1	3623.87			
10/21/93		SExit	1	3650.13		−26.26	1670.57
10/21/93		Buy	1	3650.13			
10/26/93		LExit	1	3670.81		20.68	1691.25
10/26/93		Sell	1	3670.81			
10/28/93		SExit	1	3668.30		2.51	1693.76
10/28/93		Buy	1	3668.30			
10/29/93		LExit	1	3686.74		18.44	1712.20
10/29/93		Sell	1	3686.74			
11/01/93		SExit	1	3673.33		13.41	1725.61
11/01/93		Buy	1	3673.33			
11/04/93		LExit	1	3655.72		−17.61	1708.00
11/04/93		Sell	1	3655.72			
11/08/93		SExit	1	3648.18		7.54	1715.54
11/08/93		Buy	1	3648.18			
11/15/93		LExit	1	3684.23		36.05	1751.59

* In Dow Jones Industrial points, not dollars.

NDX–SPX *DWI X S–Daily 01/02/91–11/30/94

Date	Time	Type	Cnts	Price	Signal Name	Entry P/L*	Cumulative*
11/15/93		Sell	1	3684.23			
11/24/93		SExit	1	3678.64		5.59	1757.18
11/24/93		Buy	1	3678.64			
11/30/93		LExit	1	3678.36		−0.28	1756.90
11/30/93		Sell	1	3678.36			
12/01/93		SExit	1	3707.70		−29.34	1727.56
12/01/93		Buy	1	3707.70			
12/07/93		LExit	1	3718.60		10.90	1738.46
12/07/93		Sell	1	3718.60			
12/16/93		SExit	1	3728.38		−9.78	1728.68
12/16/93		Buy	1	3728.38			
12/17/93		LExit	1	3725.58		−2.80	1725.88
12/17/93		Sell	1	3725.58			
12/21/93		SExit	1	3751.85		−26.27	1699.61
12/21/93		Buy	1	3751.85			
12/22/93		LExit	1	3753.81		1.96	1701.57
12/22/93		Sell	1	3753.81			
12/27/93		SExit	1	3768.90		−15.09	1686.48
12/27/93		Buy	1	3768.90			
12/28/93		LExit	1	3789.58		20.68	1707.16
12/28/93		Sell	1	3789.58			
12/29/93		SExit	1	3794.61		−5.03	1702.13
12/29/93		Buy	1	3794.61			
01/04/94		LExit	1	3739.16		−55.45	1646.68
01/04/94		Sell	1	3739.16			
01/05/94		SExit	1	3789.53		−50.37	1596.31
01/05/94		Buy	1	3789.53			
01/10/94		LExit	1	3824.42		34.89	1631.20
01/10/94		Sell	1	3824.42			
01/12/94		SExit	1	3855.10		−30.68	1600.52
01/12/94		Buy	1	3855.10			
01/19/94		LExit	1	3866.64		11.54	1612.06
01/19/94		Sell	1	3866.64			

* In Dow Jones Industrial points, not dollars.

NDX–SPX *DWI X S–Daily 01/02/91–11/30/94

Date	Time	Type	Cnts	Price	Signal Name	Entry P/L*	Cumulative*
01/21/94		SExit	1	3895.34		−28.70	1583.36
01/21/94		Buy	1	3895.34			
01/26/94		LExit	1	3893.09		−2.25	1581.11
01/26/94		Sell	1	3893.09			
01/31/94		SExit	1	3958.10		−65.01	1516.10
01/31/94		Buy	1	3958.10			
02/01/94		LExit	1	3976.67		18.57	1534.67
02/01/94		Sell	1	3976.67			
02/08/94		SExit	1	3919.54		57.13	1591.80
02/08/94		Buy	1	3919.54			
02/14/94		LExit	1	3894.50		−25.04	1566.76
02/14/94		Sell	1	3894.50			
02/15/94		SExit	1	3911.38		−16.88	1549.88
02/15/94		Buy	1	3911.38			
02/23/94		LExit	1	3911.66		0.28	1550.16
02/23/94		Sell	1	3911.66			
02/25/94		SExit	1	3850.88		60.78	1610.94
02/25/94		Buy	1	3850.88			
03/03/94		LExit	1	3829.49		−21.39	1589.55
03/03/94		Sell	1	3829.49			
03/04/94		SExit	1	3830.90		−1.41	1588.14
03/04/94		Buy	1	3830.90			
03/09/94		LExit	1	3853.97		23.07	1611.21
03/09/94		Sell	1	3853.97			
03/15/94		SExit	1	3863.41		−9.44	1601.77
03/15/94		Buy	1	3863.41			
03/21/94		LExit	1	3878.38		14.97	1616.74
03/21/94		Sell	1	3878.38			
03/24/94		SExit	1	3849.88		28.50	1645.24
03/24/94		Buy	1	3849.88			
03/25/94		LExit	1	3827.13		−22.75	1622.49
03/25/94		Sell	1	3827.13			
03/31/94		SExit	1	3639.71		187.42	1809.91

* In Dow Jones Industrial points, not dollars.

NDX–SPX *DWI X S–Daily 01/02/91–11/30/94

Date	Time	Type	Cnts	Price	Signal Name	Entry P/L*	Cumulative*
03/31/94		Buy	1	3639.71			
04/05/94		LExit	1	3649.50		9.79	1819.70
04/05/94		Sell	1	3649.50			
04/06/94		SExit	1	3683.18		−33.68	1786.02
04/06/94		Buy	1	3683.18			
04/07/94		LExit	1	3685.20		2.02	1788.04
04/07/94		Sell	1	3685.20			
04/18/94		SExit	1	3661.17		24.03	1812.07
04/18/94		Buy	1	3661.17			
04/19/94		LExit	1	3620.12		−41.05	1771.02
04/19/94		Sell	1	3620.12			
04/22/94		SExit	1	3662.95		−42.83	1728.19
04/22/94		Buy	1	3662.95			
04/29/94		LExit	1	3664.14		1.19	1729.38
04/29/94		Sell	1	3664.14			
05/03/94		SExit	1	3709.65		−45.51	1683.87
05/03/94		Buy	1	3709.65			
05/04/94		LExit	1	3715.00		5.35	1689.22
05/04/94		Sell	1	3715.00			
05/05/94		SExit	1	3707.27		7.73	1696.95
05/05/94		Buy	1	3707.27			
05/09/94		LExit	1	3648.97		−58.30	1638.65
05/09/94		Sell	1	3648.97			
05/19/94		SExit	1	3729.51		−80.54	1558.11
05/19/94		Buy	1	3729.51			
05/26/94		LExit	1	3754.68		25.17	1583.28
05/26/94		Sell	1	3754.68			
05/31/94		SExit	1	3746.37		8.31	1591.59
05/31/94		Buy	1	3746.37			
06/02/94		LExit	1	3770.68		24.31	1615.90
06/02/94		Sell	1	3770.68			
06/03/94		SExit	1	3749.14		21.54	1637.44
06/03/94		Buy	1	3749.14			

* In Dow Jones Industrial points, not dollars.

NDX–SPX *DWI X S–Daily 01/02/91–11/30/94

Date	Time	Type	Cnts	Price	Signal Name	Entry P/L*	Cumulative*
06/06/94		LExit	I	3782.37		33.23	1670.67
06/06/94		Sell	I	3782.37			
06/07/94		SExit	I	3758.06		24.31	1694.98
06/07/94		Buy	I	3758.06			
06/08/94		LExit	I	3765.75		7.69	1702.67
06/08/94		Sell	I	3765.75			
06/13/94		SExit	I	3764.41		1.34	1704.01
06/13/94		Buy	I	3764.41			
06/14/94		LExit	I	3790.09		25.68	1729.69
06/14/94		Sell	I	3790.09			
06/15/94		SExit	I	3817.05		−26.96	1702.73
06/15/94		Buy	I	3817.05			
06/17/94		LExit	I	3807.53		−9.52	1693.21
06/17/94		Sell	I	3807.53			
06/23/94		SExit	I	3725.09		82.44	1775.65
06/23/94		Buy	I	3725.09			
06/24/94		LExit	I	3690.85		−34.24	1741.41
06/24/94		Sell	I	3690.85			
06/27/94		SExit	I	3622.05		68.80	1810.21
06/27/94		Buy	I	3622.05			
06/30/94		LExit	I	3668.99		46.94	1857.15
06/30/94		Sell	I	3668.99			
07/01/94		SExit	I	3654.42		14.57	1871.72
07/01/94		Buy	I	3654.42			
07/05/94		LExit	I	3640.18		−14.24	1857.48
07/05/94		Sell	I	3640.18			
07/08/94		SExit	I	3674.50		−34.32	1823.16
07/08/94		Buy	I	3674.50			
07/11/94		LExit	I	3718.53		44.03	1867.19
07/11/94		Sell	I	3718.53			
07/12/94		SExit	I	3705.25		13.28	1880.47
07/12/94		Buy	I	3705.25			
07/15/94		LExit	I	3734.71		29.46	1909.93

* In Dow Jones Industrial points, not dollars.

NDX–SPX *DWI X S–Daily 01/02/91–11/30/94

Date	Time	Type	Cnts	Price	Signal Name	Entry P/L*	Cumulative*
07/15/94		Sell	1	3734.71			
07/22/94		SExit	1	3742.16		−7.45	1902.48
07/22/94		Buy	1	3742.16			
07/26/94		LExit	1	3733.09		−9.07	1893.41
07/26/94		Sell	1	3733.09			
08/01/94		SExit	1	3767.09		−34.00	1859.41
08/01/94		Buy	1	3767.09			
08/03/94		LExit	1	3788.78		21.69	1881.10
08/03/94		Sell	1	3788.78			
08/05/94		SExit	1	3745.07		43.71	1924.81
08/05/94		Buy	1	3745.07			
08/15/94		LExit	1	3774.21		29.14	1953.95
08/15/94		Sell	1	3774.21			
08/16/94		SExit	1	3767.41		6.80	1960.75
08/16/94		Buy	1	3767.41			
08/17/94		LExit	1	3798.49		31.08	1991.83
08/17/94		Sell	1	3798.49			
08/18/94		SExit	1	3769.68		28.81	2020.64
08/18/94		Buy	1	3769.68			
08/22/94		LExit	1	3744.43		−25.25	1995.39
08/22/94		Sell	1	3744.43			
08/23/94		SExit	1	3758.02		−13.59	1981.80
08/23/94		Buy	1	3758.02			
08/25/94		LExit	1	3840.58		82.56	2064.36
08/25/94		Sell	1	3840.58			
08/26/94		SExit	1	3849.97		−9.39	2054.97
08/26/94		Buy	1	3849.97			
08/30/94		LExit	1	3900.47		50.50	2105.47
08/30/94		Sell	1	3900.47			
08/31/94		SExit	1	3907.92		−7.45	2098.02
08/31/94		Buy	1	3907.92			
09/01/94		LExit	1	3899.50		−8.42	2089.60
09/01/94		Sell	1	3899.50			

* In Dow Jones Industrial points, not dollars.

NDX–SPX *DWI X S–Daily 01/02/91–11/30/94

Date	Time	Type	Cnts	Price	Signal Name	Entry P/L*	Cumulative*
09/06/94		SExit	1	3885.24		14.26	2103.86
09/06/94		Buy	1	3885.24			
09/12/94		LExit	1	3874.14		−11.10	2092.76
09/12/94		Sell	1	3874.14			
09/14/94		SExit	1	3877.17		−3.03	2089.73
09/14/94		Buy	1	3877.17			
09/15/94		LExit	1	3898.03		20.86	2110.59
09/15/94		Sell	1	3898.03			
09/16/94		SExit	1	3915.86		−17.83	2092.76
09/16/94		Buy	1	3915.86			
09/20/94		LExit	1	3920.57		4.71	2097.47
09/20/94		Sell	1	3920.57			
09/21/94		SExit	1	3875.82		44.75	2142.22
09/21/94		Buy	1	3875.82			
09/22/94		LExit	1	3863.37		−12.45	2129.77
09/22/94		Sell	1	3863.37			
09/23/94		SExit	1	3840.16		23.21	2152.98
09/23/94		Buy	1	3840.16			
09/26/94		LExit	1	3833.09		−7.07	2145.91
09/26/94		Sell	1	3833.09			
09/30/94		SExit	1	3856.98		−23.89	2122.02
09/30/94		Buy	1	3856.98			
10/04/94		LExit	1	3850.59		−6.39	2115.63
10/04/94		Sell	1	3850.59			
10/06/94		SExit	1	3788.68		61.91	2177.54
10/06/94		Buy	1	3788.68			
10/07/94		LExit	1	3773.88		−14.80	2162.74
10/07/94		Sell	1	3773.88			
10/10/94		SExit	1	3811.22		−37.34	2125.40
10/10/94		Buy	1	3811.22			
10/13/94		LExit	1	3914.51		103.29	2228.69
10/13/94		Sell	1	3914.51			
10/19/94		SExit	1	3908.79		5.72	2234.41

* In Dow Jones Industrial points, not dollars.

NDX–SPX *DWI X S–Daily 01/02/91–11/30/94

Date	Time	Type	Cnts	Price	Signal Name	Entry P/L*	Cumulative*
10/19/94		Buy	I	3908.79			
10/24/94		LExit	I	3892.98		−15.81	2218.60
10/24/94		Sell	I	3892.98			
10/25/94		SExit	I	3830.06		62.92	2281.52
10/25/94		Buy	I	3830.06			
10/26/94		LExit	I	3866.74		36.68	2318.20
10/26/94		Sell	I	3866.74			
10/27/94		SExit	I	3858.66		8.08	2326.28
10/27/94		Buy	I	3858.66			
10/28/94		LExit	I	3875.82		17.16	2343.44
10/28/94		Sell	I	3875.82			
11/01/94		SExit	I	3892.98		−17.16	2326.28
11/01/94		Buy	I	3892.98			
11/04/94		LExit	I	3855.63		−37.35	2288.93
11/04/94		Sell	I	3855.63			
11/09/94		SExit	I	3867.41		−11.78	2277.15
11/09/94		Buy	I	3867.41			
11/11/94		LExit	I	3813.92		−53.49	2223.66
11/11/94		Sell	I	3813.92			
11/14/94		SExit	I	3808.87		5.05	2228.71
11/14/94		Buy	I	3808.87			
11/23/94		LExit	I	3660.50		−148.37	2080.34
11/23/94		Sell	I	3660.50			
11/28/94		SExit	I	3708.95		−48.45	2031.89
11/28/94		Buy	I	3708.95			

Reprinted with permission of Omega Research Inc.

* In Dow Jones Industrial points, not dollars.

•

•

•

•

•

Glossary

advance-decline lines. The difference between each day's advancing issues and declining issues.

advancing issues. A measure of the total number of stocks that closed up for the day.

ask. The price at which a security is offered for sale.

bar chart. A graphical price display of a security's open, high, low, and close. Time is measured on the horizontal axis, and the value of the variable is measured on the vertical axis.

bear market. A market in which prices continue to make new lows.

bear spreads. A spread that will theoretically increase in value with a decline in the price of the underlying contract.

bid. An offer to buy at a specific price.

bull market. A market in which prices continue to make new highs.

bull spreads. A spread that will theoretically increase in value with a rise in the price of the underlying security.

call. An option contract that permits the holder to purchase a fixed amount of a specific asset at a predetermined price within a specified period of time.

cash market. A market where the actual commodity/security is bought and sold on a negotiated basis.

CBOE OEX Volatility Index (VIX). An index that reflects a market consensus estimate of future volatility, based on "at-the-money" quotes of the OEX index options.

commercial. Typically, a company/institution that hedges in the commodity markets because it uses the commodity in production of goods.

Connors-Hayward Advance-Decline Trading Pattern (CHADTP). An indicator that identifies short- and intermediate-term overbought and oversold conditions for the stock market.

contract month. The month in which a futures contract ceases trading and requires delivery of the commodity.

day order. An order to buy or sell a security that expires at the close of the trading day on which it is entered.

day trader. A speculator who takes market positions and offsets those positions by the close of the same trading day.

declining issues. A measure of the total number of stocks that closed down for the day.

delayed opening. The intentional postponement of the opening of a security. Usually the result of an unexpected development before the opening that causes an influx of buy or sell orders.

fair value. The fair value for an index futures contract equals the price of the underlying assets.

gap openings. A gap up opening occurs when today's open is greater than yesterday's high. A gap down opening occurs when today's open is less than yesterday's low.

Globex. The electronic trading exchange developed by the Chicago Mercantile Exchange.

historical volatility. The standard deviation of the logarithmic price changes measured at regular intervals of time.

implied volatility. A mathematical calculation of volatility using the actual market prices of an option contract and one of a number of pricing models.

index option. A put or call option whose underlying asset is an index.

inside day. A day in which the high is less than the previous day's high, and the low is greater than the previous day's low.

market order. An order executed at the best possible price at the time the order reaches the floor.

Market-On-Close (M.O.C.). An order filled at the current market prices near the close of the trading day.

momentum/growth stock. A speculative stock that is expected to grow at a fast rate. Typically trades at a high price/earnings ratio.

Nasdaq 100 (NDX). A capitalization-weighted index of the 100 largest OTC stocks.

option. A contract that gives the owner the right to purchase or sell an asset at a predetermined price until a specific date. A call option permits the owner to purchase an asset, and a put option permits the owner to sell an asset.

order imbalance. An excess of buy or sell orders that makes it impossible to match one type of order with its opposite. Typically occurs after unexpected news/event.

out-of-the-money. An option with no intrinsic value in terms of the relationship between the strike price and the current price of the underlying security.

overbought. A subjective view that prices have risen to an unreasonable level.

oversold. A subjective view that prices have fallen to an unreasonable level.

price persistency. Continued strength or weakness of price movement in a market.

scalper. A speculator who attempts to profit on relatively small price changes.

sector index. A weighted index of a group of securities that share certain common characteristics.

short. A position resulting from the sale of a contract.

specialist. A market maker who has the exclusive rights to make a market in a specific security.

speculator. An investor willing to assume higher risk in return of higher returns.

stop order. An order to buy or sell at the market if the market trades at or through a specified price. A sell stop order is entered below the current market. A buy stop order is entered above the current market.

stop-limit order. An order to buy or sell at a specific price or better if the market trades at or through a specific price.

straddle. The purchase of a call and a put with the same expiration and strike price.

strike price. The price that the security is delivered if exercised.

standard deviation. Square root of the variance that gauges the spread of a distribution and risk by measuring how certain we are that the return will be close to its expected value.

tick. The minimum price change in a security or contract.

trailing stop. A stop that is arbitrarily moved in order to lock in profits while allowing your position to run.

undeniable. A reversal pattern used to identify turning points in stock indexes.

volatility. The degree at which the price of an underlying instrument tends to fluctuate over time.

write. The act of selling an option.

•
•
•
•
•

Index

-
-
-
-
-

Free Report

Larry Connors and Blake Hayward have prepared a new report entitled, *Successful Trading Strategies to Exploit the Financial Media.*

To receive your free copy of this report, send your name and address to:

> Oceanview Financial Research, Inc.
> 6243 Tapia Drive
> Malibu, CA 90265
> - or -
> FAX: 310-589-2905

Your copy will be mailed immediately.